Why GOD? ✝

A 4o-Day Devotional Guide

Mitchell Morrison

Kendall Hunt
publishing company

www.kendallhunt.com
Send all inquiries to:
4050 Westmark Drive
Dubuque, IA 52004-1840

Glory to God.

I'm inspired by my wife Elizabeth and kids. Thank you for our life together!

Thank you Curtis Ross for listening to my crazy pitch.

Grateful for faithful family, friends, and colleagues who shared thoughts, prayers, and encouragement. God answers His question of "why" through your love and faithfulness.

For my Spring 2020 AVIA 300 students: Thanks for going through the 40-Days scriptures with me. Your heart to serve each other makes me smile. I hope years down the road you still check in with your wingman.

Contents

Introduction

Our steadfast God gently guides us. Not audibly, but with a faithful, consistent heart, He makes a way. He shows up every time without fail.

During early 2020, I began work on a seven-chapter aviation safety textbook. How much further apart, in terms of things to work on, could I be? Between flight safety imperatives and sensing God's voice in my life? Having wanted to create a series of embedded devotions in the safety text, an amazing thing happened as I began writing. Rather than researching aviation cases and practices, the Holy Spirit stirred deep within me. I kept going back to the verses and their meaning. How do they fit together, and what does it mean to me?

Day by day, week by week, I quickly had the beginnings of a 40-day matrix of core thoughts. Filling in mind map slots, it became clearer to me how the idea would work. Starting with Day one, I introduced the themes to my class of growing difference makers. They responded with favor and support. Several reported our "wingman conversation" was *the* highlight during their week.

* * *

When I summoned the thought and courage to pitch the idea to my publishing contact, I figured he would tell me I was crazy. But when God moves, nothing is impossible. Ask Mary.

The Senior Acquisitions Editor loved it! Who would think God could use a pilot turned professor to write a devotional series? The editor asked me to write the safety book too, but agreed to publish Why God? Eventually, this 40-day guide will accompany one or more textbooks integrating faith and specific aviation technical areas. I might write more depending on how it's received.

If you're a student in a B or D half-semester or in a semester-long term (typically 42–43 sessions), I have designed this book as your supplemental faith textbook. But I believe connecting with God transcends collegiate aviation learning. *Why God? A 40-Day Devotional* is written for *anyone* who seeks God. The format fits as a textbook, but will also bless individuals, family members, friends, study groups, and churches. Look for additional resources on the YouVersion app.

✳ ✳ ✳

When God moves, nothing is impossible.

God wants to be known and understood. He made us and knows us. Becoming satisfied by Him after waiting produces life markers. You probably have some. His blessings of old began with time itself.

Whether an old or new Christian, or a seeker, I believe God invites each person into a deep and abiding kinship with Him. My/(y)our salvation experience is a door to a new life, not just a ticket to heaven. God didn't allow His Son Jesus to die on the cross only so we could avoid hell. There's more. Much more.

Over the years, I've been blessed by so many great authors and teachers. As a life-long learner, I spend time reading scriptures and enjoy well-written prompts. My task was to integrate faith with learning for an aviation class. This book is what emerged from these efforts.

I chose the Dolphin helicopter for the cover to signify a life season during which I grew much personally, professionally, and spiritually. God shined His face upon me when leading me to serve in the U.S. Coast Guard, an honored institution rich in heritage and values.

✳ ✳ ✳

Our Heavenly Father's story to all mankind began with creation and ended with a promise of eternity. As I wrote *Why God?* I selected Bible passages based on His heart speaking to mine, through the lens of a specific framework I've conceptualized over the past several years:

Seek

Find

Know

Trust

Yield

Serve

Meet

Please join me with a foundational understanding of Biblical authority over all humanity, Jew or Gentile, man or woman, young or old, believer or non-believer, or student or teacher. I pray He will guide your journey over the next 40 days and you may connect with Him, grow in Him, and live for Him.

All scriptures are from the English Standard Version (ESV) unless otherwise noted.

Connect

Grow

Live

Devotion Framework

Each day, I provide a primary and supporting scripture—in many cases, one each from the Old and New Testaments of the Bible. I formed themes from these verses and provide them to inspire your thoughts over the coming 40 days. Use your printed Bible to read the passages and as God leads, the adjacent text as well. Follow along with your phone or tablet in the YouVersion app. Highlight the scriptures. Make notes as the Spirit leads. As the interest in the project grows, we may see a virtual community of learning based on Why God?

I have created the "Connect, Grow, Live" framework to view your position with God. Use the below prompts to guide your prayers, thoughts, and actions. It's okay to personalize the words to fit your own personality, learning style, or viewpoint. In a community of learners, share how these words (or what you adapted) connect your soul with the Creator.

 Thought tip: Schedule 15 min daily to read 40 days. Find a quiet place to spend a couple of minutes in prayer listening to God before you begin. If you want a prayer model, see the **Next Steps** section at the end of this book for a suggested prompt upon which you can build. Watch how the habit of this special and consecrated time with the Lord blesses you and those you love.

Wingman discussion. I use this technique in the classroom during presentations and in life to amplify learning of new ideas. We were created for community and iron sharpens iron. Pilots work together for safe mission accomplishment. God created a helper (Eve) for Adam. Moses had Aaron. David had Jonathan. Paul had Barnabas. Those who know me get this idea. If you don't get it now, that's okay. You will.

Who Is Your Wingman?

 Connect: Draw near and listen to God. How is He speaking to you?

Grow: Discuss today's theme with your wingman. What did you learn?

[Each day has a specific prompt.]

Live: Where will you go, what will you do, and whom will you serve? How will you live today?

Prayer: [I provide a daily prayer tailored to the specific theme. Some guests will contribute.]

My response: [Blank space for you to reflect and fill in.]

God Is—He Cares

1 Peter 5:7. Casting all your anxieties on Him, because He cares for you.

My maternal grandmother was born in 1903 and lived for 100 years. In 2000 I attended the C-130 schoolhouse at Little Rock Air Force Base in Arkansas, giving me opportunity to visit her for conversations most every weekend during a special 12-week season. By this time we had two little boys. In my thirties, I realized life was more about faith and family than achieving the brass ring. But, I was still burdened and anxious about how to balance my military career with my role as a parent. During a heartfelt conversation about parenting I'll never forget, Grandma Daisy told me, "Mitch, just love them. Tell them God cares for them and He'll never leave or forsake us. I've always loved you and your momma and daddy." Daisy modeled love, acceptance, and encouragement.

He Strengthens Us

Eight of ten college students feel stressed and one in three suffer with symptoms of depression (1.1). What causes tension for you right now? Work, finances, debt, grades, flight ratings, or competition for the next job? In Jeremiah 17:8, God tells us not to fear when heat comes. Not *if* it comes, but *when*. If we allow Him, He strengthens us—a metaphorical tree—planted with strong roots; not anxious during drought, but continuing to bear fruit. God brings tests and trials not to crush us, but to grow us.

Gen 28:15a. Behold, I am with you and will keep you wherever you go.

(1.1) The American Institute of Stress. *Stress: An Epidemic Among College Students.* Nicole Tarsitano (September 6, 2019). Retrieved from https://www.stress.org/stress-an-epidemic-among-college-students

Connect: Draw near and listen to God. How is He speaking to you?

Grow: Discuss today's theme with your wingman. What are you stressed about? How can you draw upon your life experiences to cope?

Live: Where will you go, what will you do, and whom will you serve? How will you live today?

Prayer: Lord, thank You for people who love us, like Grandma Daisy. Your love shines through in our lives through them. May we be grateful for trials and tests You bring upon our lives. Allow us to learn and grow, Lord, then go. In Jesus' name, Amen.

My response:

Connect

Grow

Live

Seek and Delight in Him

Matthew 7:7. Ask, and it will be given to you; seek, and you will find; knock, and it will be opened to you.

Okay, I'll admit it, I like baseball. No, I really like it, to the point of delight. I waited so long for my Angels' 2002 World Series game-seven victory following a rollercoaster game-six comeback after being down 6-0. We'd lost to the Brewers in 1982 despite leading two games to none. In 1986, we blew a three-run ninth-inning lead over the Red Sox in game five at home, three outs away from our first series berth. Who knows why I invest so much passion and interest in a game? Aviation invokes delight too. If you've ever flown over an expansive city on a cloudless night (Mexico City and Los Angeles come to mind) or experienced the beauty of a quiet sunrise, you know what I'm talking about. But what about eternal delight in God?

He Will Give You the Desires of Your Heart

Jesus taught us in the parable of the sower: To hear the Word and hold it fast in an honest and pure heart. As we seek Him, we find His words beckoning us to choose how to live. As we ask Him in prayer to give us understanding, God is steadfast to provide His continued Word, presence, and wisdom. Our part is to look and listen—kind of like following our favorite team during a pennant stretch. When we approach Him with our heart, He opens up new realms of desire and opportunity: His, not ours. Will you ask Him to join you in your life journey?

Psalm 37:4. Delight yourself in the Lord and He will give you the desires of your heart.

Connect: Draw near and listen to God. How is He speaking to you?

Grow: Discuss today's theme with your wingman. Think about your team, an academic achievement, or family highlight: Compare delight on earth with eternal connection to God.

Live: Where will you go, what will you do, and whom will you serve? How will you live today?

Prayer: Lord, thank You for the blessings of life. Victories that bring delight and joy in the temporal life. Would You give me understanding of Your delight, God? I knock at Your door, would You open up Your path for my life? Give me the desires of Your heart for me. I pray in Jesus' name, Amen.

My response:

Connect

Grow

Live

Acknowledge Him in Prayer

Proverbs 3:5-6. Trust in the Lord with all your heart, and do not lean on your own understanding. In all your ways acknowledge him, and he will make straight your paths.

One of my most esteemed life mentors was Retired Navy Master Chief Jim Crismon. The last time I saw Papa Jim, we sat for a while to talk about my new career as an aeronautics professor and ministry with the students. Jim was weak and thin, a mere shell of the strong, fit man with whom I had played golf and lived life. In church, Jim helped me grow as a man of faith. A patriarch, he modeled to me how to love family, including a special gift: His secret of how to bake biscuits from scratch, a holiday favorite.

We spoke about our shared heritage as military veterans. I told Jim about our new life in Virginia and thanked him for the stirring video he shared for my Coast Guard retirement ceremony. He wasn't healthy enough to make the long transcontinental flight. When our visit closed, Master Chief gave me a lone sailor pin and confirmed I could render a proper military salute.

Then he gently said, "Why don't we have a short prayer time together?" I was honored to bow to our Father in prayer with Jim and Cori.

I don't remember a lot of what we said in that prayer, but remember feeling gratitude for knowing Jim, confidence of seeing him again in heaven, and peace in trusting Christ as Jim modeled. I drove away from the Crismon's house in tears. Jim went home to be with the Lord a few weeks later.

Why Don't We Have a Short Prayer Time Together?

Jesus took time away to pray and God provided. Christ taught us to pour out our hearts to God, acknowledging His authority over us. by telling Him what we need, asking Him to hear us, and affirming our love for Him. I believe our Heavenly Father listens and responds with a daily measure of grace and strength, like Jim did when seeing an old friend one last time. Cori sent me a card with a special gift a few months after Jim died — one of his red baking aprons. Printed in white on the front: Got biscuits? (3.1)

Mark 1:35. In the early morning, while it was still dark, Jesus got up, left the house, and went away to a secluded place and was praying there.

(3.1) Card from Cori Crismon, dated December 29, 2017.

Connect: Draw near and listen to God. How is He speaking to you?

Grow: Discuss today's theme with your wingman. Who has modeled prayer for you? How can you grow in your prayer life?

Live: Where will you go, what will you do, and whom will you serve? How will you live today?

Prayer: Dear God, I acknowledge Your authority over my life and trust You. Will You hear me as I pour out my heart to You in need? Give me strength, grace, and wisdom to discern how I can walk closer with You. Thank You, Lord, for role models like Papa Jim. Allow me to leave a legacy for my family, to model Christ, and bless others like Master Chief. In Jesus' name, Amen.

My response:

Connect

Grow

Live

The Way—Wings of Refuge

John 14:6. Jesus said to him, "I am the way, and the truth, and the life. No one comes to the Father except through me."

In 2008, pilot certificates in the United States changed from heavy paper to plastic (4.1). Designers used a family portrait of the Wright Brothers as the centerpiece along with graphics of the first flight and a modern jet. Orville flew the first flight; Wilbur flew the longest of the day (4.2). That December 19, 1903 event changed the trajectory of life on earth.

For the pilots, get your FAA certificate and look at it. Orville had the mustache, Wilbur was bald.

When did you go on your first solo flight? Mine was in February, 1983 at a stage field near Fort Rucker, Alabama in a TH-55A helicopter.

Take Shelter under His Wing

Whether we serve in aviation or not, life is a collection of countless small things with guiding moments bounded by memorable seasons marked by few events defining our path. We have a way in Jesus, a refuge in God, and a power source in the Holy Spirit. When did you decide to trust Christ? Have you experienced a crisis of faith? Was there a time in your life when you saw God's hand clear at work? I don't think it has to be an earth-shattering thing. Little things come from our Heavenly Father too. Take shelter under His wing.

Ruth 2:12. The Lord repay you for what you have done, and a full reward be given you by the Lord, the God of Israel, under whose wings you have come to take refuge.

(4.1) Aircraft Owners and Pilots Association news, February 28, 2008.

(4.2) National Park Service. Retrieved from https://www.nps.gov/articles/firstflight.htm

Connect: Draw near and listen to God. How is He speaking to you?

Grow: Discuss today's theme with your wingman. Have you seen God's hand at work? Describe a big event and a small thing.

Live: Where will you go, what will you do, and whom will you serve? How will you live today?

Prayer: Lord, You created the skies that both the Wright brothers flew in and we fly in today. Thank You for the big and small life events where we notice Your hand at work. May we never grow weary of resting in Your shadow. Jesus, show us the way for life. We're grateful to fly in Your world, O God. In Christ's name, Amen.

My response:

Connect

Grow

Live

Hope—Future—Calling

Jeremiah 29:11. For I know the plans I have for you, declares the Lord, plans for welfare and not for evil, to give you a future and a hope.

In 1956, two modern four-engined airliners departed Los Angeles Eastbound toward their destinations in the Midwest. With Eisenhower's economy on the upswing, the sky was expansive and commercial aviation booming. Instead of a grueling automobile trip, travelers from California could reach Kansas City or Chicago in one day. The Trans World Airlines Super Constellation collided in midair over the Grand Canyon with the United Airlines Douglas DC-7, killing all 128 occupants on both aircraft (5.1).

United States Government investigators' findings led to legislation for Congress appropriating more than a quarter billion dollars to revamp the federal air transportation infrastructure. Upgrades included ground-based radio aids, air traffic control radar facilities, and a newly regulated high-altitude airspace system. These plans gave travelers hope that future tragedies would be averted. New transportation improvements include satellite-based navigation, standardized digital communications, and data sharing to discern trends.

Your Future Good

Things happen in our life for a reason. They capture our attention so we can understand the bigger picture. We shake ourselves out of tragedy and move ahead. For me, a major event in my life was my parents' divorce when I was a teenager. It took several years for me to see and understand God's hand and forgive the hurt. But God was faithful to allow me to move beyond the tragedy to see His plans and future for me. He will be faithful to show you His calling upon your life too.

God has a plan for all of us. Draw near to Him.

Romans 8:28. And we know that for those who love God all things work together for good, for those who are called according to His purpose.

(5.1) Wilson & Binnema (2014). *Managing Risk.* Newcastle, WA: Aviation Supplies & Academics, Inc.

Connect: Draw near and listen to God. How is He speaking to you?

Grow: Discuss today's theme with your wingman. What tragedy have you experienced or seen that you have learned from?

Live: Where will you go, what will you do, and whom will you serve? How will you live today?

Prayer: Dear Lord, I've had a tough road healing from my parents' divorce [or other hurt you may substitute], but thank You for having a plan of good and a future for me. I ask for wisdom to discern Your calling so I may be able to grow in Your purpose for my life. You remain faithful and steadfast to provide hope for me and those I love. I praise and honor You for Your promise, and trust You moving forward. I ask these things in Jesus' name. Amen.

My response:

Connect

Grow

Live

Heart and Soul

Deuteronomy 4:29. But from there you will seek the Lord your God and you will find Him, if you search after Him with all your heart and with all your soul.

Most people want to find deeper fulfillment in life beyond wealth or accolade. Our life journey includes a start, middle, and finish. During my early career, two friends crashed after hitting wires while on an OH-58C helicopter night-vision goggle training mission.

First Lieutenant Byron Bellamy was newly assigned to our unit. Eager to learn, the Lieutenant led with energy and purpose. That night I sat in the right seat as a Pilot in Command under instruction with an experienced trainer. Our Troop Commander accompanied us in the back of our ship. We received a frantic radio call about the crash and landed near the site. In darkness, the Major walked from our running helicopter to assess what had happened. He returned shortly and said grimly, "Lieutenant Bellamy is dead."

Losing my platoon leader seemed unfair. After college, officer candidate training, and flight school, Byron motivated us with quiet purpose. One day I struggled with how to finish a project involving several other soldiers. The Lieutenant took time to talk with me and mentored, not commanded, me in handling the task.

Seeking Relationship

Byron didn't have an opportunity to plan the ending chapter of his life that night, however, I believe he finished well. The Lieutenant took me under his wing and taught me to lead by relationship rather than issuing orders. I compare Bellamy's gentle style with Jesus, who tells us we can learn from Him to find rest. Another lasting memory of Bellamy: His infectious smile.

Matthew 11:29. Take my yoke upon you, and learn from me, for I am gentle and lowly in heart, and you will find rest for your souls.

Connect: Draw near and listen to God. How is He speaking to you?

Grow: Discuss today's theme with your wingman. Do you see heart and soul in others and receive blessing?

Live: Where will you go, what will you do, and whom will you serve? How will you live today?

Prayer: Dear Heavenly Father, we don't know when our finish will come, but allow us to experience fulfillment in our lives beyond wealth or accolade. Thank You, God, for the blessing to know and learn from First Lieutenant Byron Bellamy, who took me under his wing with purpose and encouragement. Byron's gentle smile made a difference for me as I learned how to lead soldiers and grow as an example for others. In the memory of Byron and to honor his legacy, may I make my life matter, and honor You Lord, by lifting up someone else. My soul rests in You! I pray in Jesus' name, Amen.

My response:

Connect

Grow

Live

Mercy and Compassion

Isaiah 30:18. Therefore the Lord waits to be gracious to you, and therefore He exalts Himself to show mercy to you. For the Lord is a God of justice; blessed are all those who wait for Him.

Have you ever had intense desire to have something, but it seemed just out of reach? At the age of 19 my family couldn't afford college. We certainly didn't have funds to pursue my goal of flying. The TV commercial said, "The Army is the only place you can go from high school to flight school!" The recruiter said, "If you can pass the test, I'll work on your package." When I got an offer and accepted the slot, my father was critical and skeptical. We had a family friend who had been a recruiter and he affirmed the program was selective and, in today's vernacular, "legit." What a moment when my dad pinned on my silver warrant officer bars and pilot wings during graduation!

Wait for Him

In Disney's classic 2004 film, *Miracle*, Coach Herb Brooks said, "Great moments are born from great opportunity. . .Tonight we are the greatest hockey team in the world! Now go out there and take it!" The Cold War had gripped America with discouragement, fear, and anxiety on the heels of Vietnam, Watergate, and the Iran hostage crisis. Winning the gold medal brought a sense of transformational momentum during a season where people were harassed, helpless, and without hope (7.1). Under President Reagan's buildup era, I was a fortunate recipient of opportunity to become a military helicopter pilot. But I had to go out there and take it.

Matthew 9:36. When He saw the crowds, He had compassion for them, because they were harassed and helpless, like sheep without a shepherd.

(7.1) O'Connor, G. (Director), & Guggenheim, E. (Written by). (2004). *Miracle* [Motion Picture]. United States: Disney.

Connect: Draw near and listen to God. How is He speaking to you today? What desires has He placed on your heart?

Grow: Discuss today's theme with your wingman. What are you working on, and how will God be gracious and show mercy to you?

Live: Where will you go, what will you do, and whom will you serve? How will you live today?

Prayer: Lord, thank You for Your steadfast timing that never fails. Jesus, You looked upon the crowds with compassion. I'm in the middle of them today. See me and be my Shepherd. I wait for Your hand. In Jesus' name, Amen.

My response:

Connect

Grow

Live

God's Name and Voice

Revelation 3:20. Behold I stand at the door and knock. If anyone hears my voice and opens the door, I will come in to him and eat with him, and he with me.

I don't know about you, but God's voice doesn't appear audibly to me. His gentle whispers come in the form of spiritual promptings, revelations of themes from scriptures, and circumstances. On February 2, 1943, a B-25 medium bomber, serial number 129828, crashed at 9:40 on a Tuesday night at Sharp Top Mountain near Bedford, Virginia. I would like to hear the voice of the 22-year-old pilot Second Lieutenant Paul Pitts from rural East Oklahoma (8.1) — his story, hopes, dreams, and life goals as he and his young crew neared their time to join the fight against fascist tyranny.

In 2001, the town of Bedford dedicated a memorial to the five brave men lost that night. The Virginia state assembly declared February 2 a day to remember lost aircrews (8.1). According to archived military records, #129828 was one of seven fatal and 59 overall stateside Army Air Corps crashes occurring on February 2, 1943 alone (8.2). It strikes me how many mishaps occurred on just a single day, but signifies the massive undertaking of training and logistics required in the midst of winning World War II. How can we win in our fight against forces in the spiritual realm?

God wants to be heard; but leaves the choice to us to call upon Him and listen through promptings of the Holy Spirit, scripture, and circumstances. Knowing it's God is the first step of listening for Him. Early in the Bible, Adam and Eve's son, Seth, had a son and men began to pray: *"To Seth also a son was born, and he called his name Enosh. At that time men began to call upon the name of the Lord." (Genesis 4:26)*

Pharaoh told Moses, "I do not know the Lord." It may sound trite, but the realist in me thinks, "Good luck with that!" I think we've all tried doing things our own way instead of God's. Things didn't work very well for

(8.1) ABC Television Channel 13 News story (January 31, 2013). Retrieved from https://wset.com/archive/the-sharp-top-tragedy-70-years-later

(8.2) Army Air Corps Records. Retrieved from https://www.aviationarchaeology.com/src/AARmonthly/Feb1943S.htm

(8.3) Paul M. Pitts. Retrieved from https://www.findagrave.com/memorial/14149756/paul-morrow-pitts

Pharaoh, and I can confirm the same in my life when I refused to listen to God. Listen to God's voice. And honor fallen heroes like Paul Pitts (8.3).

Exodus 5:2. But Pharaoh said, "Who is the Lord that I should obey His voice to let Israel go? I do not know the Lord, and besides, I will not let Israel go."

 Connect: Draw near and listen to God. How is He speaking to you?

Grow: Discuss today's theme with your wingman. How do you connect with God? How do you listen and watch for His prompts? In most cases, I believe the loudest He appears is through a gentle Holy Spirit whisper. How about you?

Live: Where will you go, what will you do, and whom will you serve? How will you live today?

Prayer: Lord, thank You for the legacy of heroes whose lives became shortened through tragedy, like the men from aircraft #129828. As we live, may we take time to learn from stories near our own generation. Let us learn from Your stories of old, Lord. May we never become like Pharaoh, unwilling to know You. We want to be like one of the first sons in the Bible, Seth, calling upon Your name. Let us hear Your voice! In Jesus' name, Amen.

My response:

Connect

Grow

Live

Gentleness and Life

Psalm 18:35 You have given me the shield of Your salvation, and Your right hand supported me, and Your gentleness made me great.

My wife volunteers at the middle school library. Recently they've been rehabilitating the school property, requiring their team to move their books and discard old, unused volumes. When I arrived home, I noticed *A History of Aviation* on the dining table for me. The book was donated in 1993, and was checked out just once (in 1997) over the past 27 years. Cover photos include Charles Lindbergh, Doolittle's takeoff from the USS Hornet, a Wright flyer, B-17 formation, and shuttle launch.

The author was local retired Grumman executive Peter Viemeister, a Rensselaer Polytechnic Institute scholar and Massachusetts Institute of Technology fellow. Written in 1990, this discarded book, and its connection to the local community of Bedford, Virginia, became a treasure to me. Viemeister quoted Melvin Dickler, a B-26 bombardier navigator: "I liked the feeling of belonging. I enjoyed the camaraderie, and the spirit and the sense of teamwork. We had pride in how we did our job. I liked that." Viemeister spoke of past colleagues rekindling old friendships (9.1).

I Liked the Feeling of Belonging

Buried in the final chapter were photos and stories from local families, including a young aspiring Coast Guard pilot, one of 520 to solo a vintage 1941 Piper (9.1). I appreciate how Viemeister noted the significance of an old Piper giving so many aviators their first experience in flight. How many went on to serve our nation in the military?

Back to the photo: That young guy is a colleague with whom I served! The Coast Guard provides numbers to pilots: I'm #3014 and my friend #3227. Military veterans have a special bond of shared values, devotion, and honor for each other, especially those who served together on the line or high- visibility staff roles. Even after years or decades, we reconnect and pick up where we left off in conversation. It's fun to find serendipitous connections.

Acts 17:25b. . . . since He Himself gives all mankind life and breath and everything.

(9.1) Viemeister, P. (1990). *A History of Aviation: They Were There*. Bedford, Virginia: Hamilton's.

Connect: Draw near and listen to God. How is He speaking to you?

Grow: Discuss today's theme with your wingman. Who has encouraged and inspired you to reach high and dream big? How can you give back?

Live: Where will you go, what will you do, and whom will you serve? How will you live today?

Prayer: *God, You give all things, including Your own qualities built into us. We honor those who have gone before us, who told stories to encourage us to reach high and dream big. I'm grateful, Lord, for Peter Viemeister and his obscure book published in rural Virginia. Although Mr. Viemeister has passed, his book remains, giving a connection between past and future generations. May we be inspired to lead the next generation to serve with gentleness and life. In Jesus' name, Amen.*

My response:

Connect

Grow

Live

Lost and Found

Luke 15:24. For this my son was dead and is alive again; he was lost, and is found. And they began to celebrate.

At 7:40 a.m. on December 7, 1941, Japanese Captain Mitsuo Fuchida's radio-man signaled: "To, To, To." Pronounced "toe, toe, toe"— short for *totsug-ekiseyo*, which translates to "charge!" — these words began a day of infamy for America's greatest generation (10.1). The U.S. fleet, facilities, and aircraft at Pearl Harbor was left in ruins with almost 4,000 dead. I visited the USS Arizona memorial and saw the black seeps of oil bubbling slowly to the surface, like teardrops from long ago.

President Roosevelt wanted to send a message to Japan, and during Doolittle's April 1942 raid, Jacob DeShazer bombed Nagoya as a B-25 bombardier. His pilot and turret gunner were executed by a firing squad, while DeShazer and three others were imprisoned by the Japanese for 40 months. Jacob convinced his captors to borrow one tattered English Bible during a three-week period in May 1944 and met Jesus, changing his heart from hatred to pity (10.2).

Years later, Jacob DeShazer returned to Japan as a missionary. Retired as a rice farmer, Mitsuo Fuchida received a gospel tract from DeShazer's ministry and prayed to the Lord, surrendering his life to Christ. Two former enemies became friends and preached a testimony of forgiveness and reconciliation to thousands all over the world.

For some, however, forgiveness remained difficult. USS Arizona survivor Don Stratton explained the steep cost to reconcile with Fuchida (10.3). God seeks to save and restore that which is lost. You haven't done enough wrong in your life to make God not want to save or forgive you. Return to Him. Pray about forgiving others who have wronged you. It could change the trajectory of your life.

2 Chronicles 30:9. For if you return to the Lord, your brothers and your children will find compassion with their captors and return to this land. For the Lord your God is gracious and merciful and will not turn away His face from you, if you return to Him.

(10.1) Fuchida, M. (1961). *From Pearl Harbor to Calvary*. Republished in 2016 by Pickle Partners Publishing.

(10.2) *The New York Times*, March 23, 2008. Retrieved from https://www.nytimes.com/ 2008/03/23/us/23deshazer.html

(10.3) Stratton, D. & Gire, K. (2016). *All the Gallant Men*. New York: HarperCollins.

Connect: Draw near and listen to God. How is He speaking to you?

Grow: Discuss today's theme with your wingman. Perhaps you know Christ, but have drifted away from His fellowship. Come back. Or like Fuchida did, you need to surrender and live for Him. Come. If you need to forgive someone, ask the Holy Spirit to help. It's difficult, if not impossible, in your own power.

Live: Where will you go, what will you do, and whom will you serve? How will you live today?

Prayer: Heavenly Father, You seek to save all who are lost, no matter the deed, big or small. You seek our open, willing, and repentant heart, not seeing our past or nationality. You want us at Your table, and yes, depending on our circumstance, we come (or come back). Allow me to forgive those who have wronged me — some recently, others decades past. It's never too late to redeem the time, Lord, in Your power and strength. Thank You Lord for stories of forgiveness and reconciliation between foes. In Jesus' name, Amen.

My response:

Connect

Grow

Live

Favor in Christ

Proverbs 8:35. For whoever finds me finds life and obtains favor with the Lord.

In 2009 in Fargo, North Dakota, the Red River swelled to double its flood level, exceeding the past record from 1897 (11.1). Workers built sandbag barriers to slow the rising waters. Although uncommon, Coast Guard disaster response efforts included our Sacramento-based C-130 unit. My crew and I launched to deliver relief supplies, with orders to return to home station that day due to limited aircraft availability.

Supplies delivered, we readied for departure, however, the flight engineer found ice and frost on the wing, fuselage, and tail during his preflight. We called for de-icing service, which took several minutes. We gave the operator our government payment card, but the charge was declined. We had just a few minutes before a four-hour flight home would adversely impact our crew day.

The parka-clad man asked the senior officer present (me) to call his supervisor. Knowing we had traveled to help the flood-stricken region, the nice lady on the phone recognized our predicament and granted us favor on behalf of the City of Fargo. "You're free to go, we can coordinate payment later!"

We already had two strikes against us — mission pressure and weather. We fought a third — fatigue from a long day of mission coordination, flight planning, and execution. We completed the Fargo leg, but became delayed and distracted by de-icing and payment details. On climb out, something just didn't seem right. The aircraft seemed mushy, and our indicated airspeed slowed.

My mind raced. Was it icing? Did we miss something? We reviewed our checklist and scanned the instrument panel. Was the anti-ice system working?

Seconds of silence passed. Suddenly the flight engineer exclaimed: "FLAPS!" Busy with a radio call, we had not retracted the flaps! Embarrassed by our mistake, we moved the flap lever, made it home safe, and reported our error and story so others could learn.

We committed an error, but we learned from it. We received favor from a nice lady in Fargo that day. In telling the story of our pressure-filled, fatigue-laden,

(11.1) News coverage from CNN. Retrieved from https://www.cnn.com/2009/US/weather/03/27/north.dakota.flooding/index.html

distraction-prone flight experience, we received grace from our leaders and colleagues who empathized, comparing mistakes they, too, had made. I'm glad I can find favor in Christ who died for my sins. I don't have to be perfect!

Romans 5:8. But God demonstrates His own love toward us, in that while we were yet sinners, Christ died for us.

 Connect: Draw near and listen to God. How is He speaking to you?

Grow: Discuss today's theme with your wingman. Have you ever felt pressure to finish a mission and made an error? How did you learn from it?

Live: Where will you go, what will you do, and whom will you serve? How will you live today?

Prayer: *Lord, thank You for Your favor that allows us to be human. While we worry about pressures, distractions, and mistakes, we have a Savior who died for our sins. We don't have to be perfect. We just need to believe. Thank You for Jesus, our Christ. It's in His precious, majestic, and holy name we ask, Amen.*

My response:

Connect

Grow

Live

New and Alive

Lamentations 3:22-23. The steadfast love of the Lord never ceases; His mercies never come to an end; they are new every morning; great is Your faithfulness.

When I was in the seventh grade, I remember seeing the transport planes land one by one, day by day, at the military base near our house in Garden Grove. I saw the news that Vietnam had fallen to the Communists, and thousands of refugees poured into Orange County.

During Mr. Hummer's Math class at Marie L. Hare Junior High, I met Don Nguyen. "M"s came before "N"s so Don was behind me. His name was spelled funny, but we learned it was simple to pronounce—"wen." Don appeared nervous on that first day. So was I, and we quickly became friends. I asked about Don's previous life, and he didn't want to talk much about the war.

He told me how much he loved America and how grateful he was for the opportunity to go to school with me and our classmates. I didn't really get it then, but he was given the gift of a new life in America.

The Vietnam War scarred many families, including the Nichols'. I knew Jimmy from church, and remember seeing him during a Wednesday night service when he visited on leave from helicopter training. He played with me, and I remember kicking him in the shin with my hard-soled wing tips. I also remember the night our pastor announced during service that Jimmy's helicopter had been shot down, and that Jimmy had died in the crash. We cried and prayed that night.

Even today, thousands of Vietnam veterans carry the wounds of defeat. In the 1970s, America integrated thousands of Vietnamese immigrants, many of whom settled in my old community, Garden Grove, California. The United States and Vietnam have normalized economic and diplomatic relations, giving opportunity for veterans and natives to visit the once war-torn country.

Only God can heal the deep scars. I'm blessed by the memories of Don Nguyen and Jimmy Nichols.

Hebrews 4:12. For the word of God is living and active, sharper than any two-edged sword, piercing to the division of soul and of spirit, or joints and of marrow, and discerning the thoughts and intentions of the heart.

Connect: Draw near and listen to God. What do you sense today? How is He speaking to you?

Grow: Discuss today's theme with your wingman. Have you met a war refugee or known a soldier who was killed in action?

Live: Where will you go, what will you do, and whom will you serve? How will you live today?

Prayer: (From John Nichols—Jimmy's brother) I come to You today Lord, thanking You for Your steadfast love and comfort You gave to me and my family at the loss of my brother, Jimmy. Having the knowledge in the scripture teachings that You would comfort those in need, we were able to make it through the dark times. Thank You Lord that every day is a new beginning and opportunity to grow and to share Your word. I pray for a refreshing of the Spirit in us each day, and to see each day as a new fresh life in You. Please continue to keep and bless us, Amen.

My response:

Connect

Grow

Live

Love (Faith, Hope)

Ephesians 3:19. And to know the love of Christ that surpasses knowledge, that you may be filled with all the fullness of God.

At the hand of my Mom's gentle prompt, I knelt on my own and prayed to God, accepting Jesus Christ as my savior when I was seven years old. Mom and I remain connected through Bible plans on the YouVersion app (she's been part of my private personal daily study group since January 2019). Like most families, mom, dad, and I have walked through both good and bad days.

During Troubled Times, We Need Faith, Hope, and Love

Mom told me about the day President John F. Kennedy died. She held me in her arms, cried, asking God to show up. During troubled times, we need faith, hope, and love. My high school in California was to be named Centralia—the Patriots. Instead, school board leaders renamed our school John F. Kennedy—the Fighting Irish. Painted on the front facade was a JFK quote: "Ask not what your country can do for you, ask what you can do for your country."

Kennedy had been a war hero, swimming away from the wreckage of his destroyed PT boat with one of his crew in tow. JFK was an inspiring leader who challenged our nation to put a man on the moon during the 1960s. On July 20, 1969, more than half a billion people watched Neil Armstrong climb down the ladder of Eagle: "That's one small step for a man, one giant leap for mankind" (13.1).

During an interview years later, Armstrong praised "hundreds of thousands" who made the lunar landing possible (13.2). From the tears of a hurting young mother to a quote painted on a wall, JFK's life and legacy made a distinct mark upon me. So did Jesus. Every year when I read through the Bible again, God's masterpiece comes alive each morning—a new treasure unfolding alive through the power of the Holy Spirit.

(13.1) NASA webpage. Retrieved from https://www.nasa.gov/mission_pages/apollo/ apollo11.html

(13.2) NASA webpage. Retrieved from https://www.nasa.gov/sites/default/files/62281main_armstrong_oralhistory.pdf

Jeremiah 33:3. Call to me and I will answer you, and will tell you great and hidden things that you have not known.

✳ ✳ ✳

 Connect: Draw near and listen to God. How is He speaking to you?

Grow: Discuss today's theme with your wingman. What stories from growing up do you remember? When did you receive Jesus?

Live: Where will you go, what will you do, and whom will you serve? How will you live today?

Prayer: *God, thank You for loving moms and dads who teach their children about Jesus Christ. We're grateful for the legacy of leaders such as JFK and Neil Armstrong—heroes who accomplished mighty things. Father, may we take courage to do those tasks that only we can do, to Your honor and glory. In Jesus' name, Amen.*

My response:

Connect

Grow

Live

Delight in Forgiveness

Jeremiah 9:24. But let him who boasts boast in this, that he understands and knows Me, that I am the Lord Who practices steadfast love, justice, and righteousness in the earth. For in these things I delight, declares, the Lord.

In 2019, my wife and I traveled with a group of faculty and leaders to Israel. While staying at a hotel in Jerusalem, we had leisurely departed the hotel in a large group and engaged in animated conversations during early evening darkness. We had traveled several stops on a train, then disembarked to various points of interest. My wife and I joined another couple for a walk after dinner, agreeing to return later on our own separate from the group.

It Was Time for Me and My Ego to Pass the Flight Controls

The time arrived for us to return to the hotel and we huddled to determine the correct route. As I pondered our options, I remembered my Google Maps app had been working and asked a passing group of uniformed Israeli soldiers to help me enter the address of the hotel. The route was clearly defined and direct. It looked good to me. Besides I'm the pilot who knows how to navigate.

As we walked and talked, enjoying the evening with Steve and Delta Keith, things began to appear different. A retired Air Force Colonel and Chaplain, Steve asked, "Are you sure, Mitch?" "Yes, I got this!" "Okay Mitch, you're the pilot!" You see what's coming next, even though I didn't. Passing more unfamiliar landmarks, we realized we were in the walled Arab quarter of the old city. Things weren't right. It was time for me and my ego to pass the flight controls. My wife got out her phone and said, "You can continue if you want, but I'm going the other way!" Fortunately, I relented, realizing the soldier had entered direct routing through areas we shouldn't go, especially at night.

It's a traditional thing I suppose. The Type A pilot always knows how to navigate, but this time, even after asking for help, I got us lost. Funny thing is I was the only one who really noticed. I felt humiliated, but instead of dwelling on it, I asked Steve, Delta, and my wife to forgive me. They were kind and tenderhearted as described in Ephesians 4:32. We all had a good laugh and created another memory of our Israel trip. Then I got on with the hard part—understanding and forgiving myself, by God's grace.

Acts 13:38-39. Let it be known to you therefore, brothers, that through this Man forgiveness of sins is proclaimed to you, and by Him everyone who believes if freed from everything from which you could not be freed by the law of Moses.

Connect: Draw near and listen to God. How is He speaking to you?

Grow: Discuss today's theme with your wingman. Have you ever been wrong and felt humiliated? Do you realize God has forgiven you? How do you need to understand yourself? In some cases, how do you need to forgive yourself?

Live: Where will you go, what will you do, and whom will you serve? How will you live today?

Prayer: (From Chaplain Steve Keith) Gracious Lord, You call us to follow and trust You with our lives and destination. You never lose Your way and always bring us home! At the same time, You call us to step out and lead, to be lights and guides in the darkness. We are joyfully confident when the opportunity avails to show others the way, but forever humbled when we fail! Still, in our embarrassment, we realize You are calling us to lead like You, to be humble servant leaders who esteem others better than ourselves. You call us to lead in all graciousness knowing there is only one perfect leader. Lord Jesus, may we seek forgiveness when we fail, delight in receiving compassion, and never stop trying to lead like You! Amen.

My response:

Connect

Grow

Live

God's Spirit at Work

2 Peter 1:20-21. Knowing this first of all, that no prophecy of Scripture comes from someone's own interpretation. For no prophecy was ever produced by the will of man, but men spoke from God as they were carried along by the Holy Spirit.

Francis Lyle Lee entered the U.S. Army Air Corps as an aviation cadet March 5, 1942. Lee began primary flight training on June 27 in the 165 hp Ryan PT-22. With 9 hours and 3 minutes of dual instruction logged, Cadet Lee soloed on his 14th flight over California's Central Valley. Frank's training journey continued in the 450 hp BT-13, 650hp AT-6, and various fighters including the P-47, P-40, and eventually the P-51 Mustang.

Lee's aviation duties during World War II took him from California to Arizona, then Tallahassee, Florida, where he continued work as a gunnery instructor and assistant operations officer. On February 28, 1945, Captain Lee departed San Francisco, bound for the Pacific theater of operations. On June 10, 1945, Lee was credited with an aerial victory over a Japanese Tony fighter while in battle over Tokyo. With 1,547 hours as a pilot, including 1,166 hours in fighter aircraft, Francis Lyle Lee returned home in late 1945 to Roanoke, Virginia (15.1).

Lee was one of millions of brave Americans who served during World War II. Frank rejoined his wife, the former Francis Gusler, and young daughter, Nancy, to attend Washington and Lee University, build a business, and leave a legacy—not as a war hero, but as a good husband, father, and granddad. According to family lore, God's spirit touched Lee with the strong hands of a builder who made great pickles (15.2). What ordinary people have had extraordinary influence upon your life?

Source: Mitchell Morrison, © Nancy Swartz

Photo with Lee and Nancy
Tallahassee, Florida: 1944.

(15.1) Conversation with Nancy Swartz and review of Lee records.

(15.2) Conversation with Julie Polk (Nancy's daughter).

Psalms 16:11. You make known to me the path of life; in your presence there is fullness of joy; at your right hand are pleasures forevermore.

 Connect: Draw near and listen to God. How is He speaking to you?

Grow: Think of an ordinary person who made a lasting impact upon your journey. Discuss today's theme with your wingman.

Live: Where will you go, what will you do, and whom will you serve? How will you live today?

Prayer: *Dear Heavenly Father, I'm grateful for the blessing of meeting Nancy Swartz and reading through the logbooks, photos, and papers from her father, Frank Lee. You connect us with people and circumstance with divine purpose and timing. Allow Captain Francis Lyle Lee's life story to inspire others. Encourage us, Lord, that each person's journey and legacy matters. Amen.*

My response:

Connect

Grow

Live

Truth in Love

John 8:32. And you will know the truth, and the truth will set you free.

In 1908, U.S. Army Lieutenant Thomas Selfridge worked with an inventor named Orville Wright to evaluate a prototype machine's ability to transform war fighting. Less than five years removed from Kitty Hawk, two brothers from Ohio continued to refine and adapt materials, construction methods, and equipment on their Wright Flyer. The War Department chose a parade ground at Fort McNair in Washington, DC for the test.

Seeking more performance, the Wrights lengthened the two symmetrical propeller blades by a few inches. After a successful bench test, the brothers placed the longer prop on the machine. Orville and Selfridge climbed aboard the aircraft, sitting side by side on the bottom wing's open space. Thomas wore a suit and hat; Orville a leather jacket and goggles.

An Anchor Point That Never Fails—Jesus Christ

With increased thrust from the new prop, they jolted forward to takeoff. The two men rose above the amazed crowd of officials and spectators. Suddenly, a popping noise occurred, the aircraft tail fluttered, then the nose dropped. The machine fell into a heap on the field, tumbled on top of the two men and came to rest upside down. Selfridge was unconscious, with a skull fracture. Wright was banged up, but coherent. Orville said that the aircraft had suddenly gone into an uncontrolled dive. The Lieutenant died later that night.

Army Signal Corps engineers conducted the first U.S. military aircraft mishap investigation. The wood, metal, wire, and fabric aircraft structure flexed under the stress of flight, leading to prop contact with a rudder guy wire and subsequent anchor point failure. The resulting loss of aircraft stability led to a center of gravity shift, thus the uncontrolled dive (16.1). The Wrights didn't have strain gauges and high definition cameras, so they had to experiment.

We have an anchor point that never fails—Jesus Christ. His truth gives life and freedom. We don't need to be religious, but love, trust, and obey Him.

The veil was torn, and our Heavenly Father no longer requires deeds of sacrifice or rituals of burnt offerings. God just wants us to grow closer to know Him. Not

(16.1) Chief Signal Officer Report. Courtesy of the Smithsonian museum.

to know of Him in our head, but to know Him at a soul level with our heart. Experience freedom that stems from real faith and belief in Jesus Christ.

Hosea 6:6. For I desire steadfast love and not sacrifice, the knowledge of God rather than burnt offerings.

 Connect: Draw near and listen to God. How is He speaking to you?

Grow: Discuss today's theme with your wingman. Have you ever experimented and failed? What is your anchor point?

Live: Where will you go, what will you do, and whom will you serve? How will you live today?

Prayer: Heavenly Father, thank You for pioneers such as Tom Selfridge and the Wrights. Their work has given us opportunity to fly safely in the skies You created. We marvel every day for new blessings and look forward to see how You lead moving forward. We want to know You with our heart, soul, and inner being, O God. Grant us Your favor and blessing. In Jesus' name, Amen.

My response:

Connect

Grow

Live

Created for Calling

Psalm 103:14. For He knows our frame; he remembers that we are dust.

In the thick fog over the Gulf of Alaska, we flew in an unlimited ceiling and zero visibility. I remember looking down at my survival suit, thinking about how long I could survive in the frigid water. We had 330 pounds of fuel, about 13 minutes until our reserve, and we were hundreds of miles away from land.

I piloted the helicopter from the left seat, my left hand on the collective monitoring the altitude. With my right thumb and forefinger, I slowly tweaked the heading bug. The horizontal situation vertical display showed the heading in increments of ones with the radar displaying the cutter in the distance. Flying a radar approach in zero/zero brought a rush of adrenaline. Time slowed to milliseconds.

When the ship was in sight, we could see the wake below and figures of the landing crew silhouetted against the hangar —not the typical sight of a small ship in the distance against the background of clear skies. We literally couldn't see the front of the ship, which was only 378 feet long.

Do You Know Your Place with God?

That day, I thought I may die of hypothermia, but was grateful for the opportunity to test my skills to the limit. The weather forecast had changed, and we had to trust our equipment, training, and team to safely land. I knew it could work, but I had to do my part. Do you know your place with God? What's your part?

Ephesians 1:18. Having the eyes of your hearts enlightened, that you may know what is the hope to which he has called you, what are the riches of his glorious inheritance in the saints.

Connect: Draw near and listen to God. How is He speaking to you?

Grow: Discuss today's theme with your wingman. Have you ever been tested to the limit in a challenging circumstance? How did God show up?

Live: Where will you go, what will you do, and whom will you serve? How will you live today?

Prayer: Dear Jesus, thank You for giving us Your glorious hope and the opportunity to know You. God the Father created us in His image, and we don't want to just know about You, we want to know Your heart, Your ways, to understand You in a deeper, more abiding way. Let us return to the days where we have really lived, and honor You with that gift. We ask in Your holy name, Amen.

My response:

Connect

Grow

Live

God's Purpose

Job 42:2. I know that You can do all things, and that no purpose of Yours can be thwarted.

On June 1, 1999, American Airlines Flight 1420 departed Dallas en route to Little Rock, Arkansas. Tad Hardin sat in seat 27D next to his friend, 22-year-old James Harrison along with others on their Ouachita Baptist University student group returning home from a European music tour. A talented vocalist, Kristin Maddox, sat in seat 28A.

Fatigued by delays, the frazzled pilots miscalculated crosswind limits and continued the approach during a driving thunderstorm. During the landing, the MD-80 slid off the runway, broke apart, and burst into flames. Tad and James unbuckled to escape the dense smoke. Tad's last memory was James asking if Tad wanted his jacket as Tad went forward to exit and James aft. James died that night, along with 10 others, including the captain performing the landing.

I Can Help Others Get Unstuck

During Flight 1420's 20-year survivors' reunion, Tad spoke with Kristin about his own physical and emotional healing from depression, anger, shattered dreams, and troubled memories. Kristin's smoke-scarred lungs prevented a dream career as a vocalist, but God created beauty from the ashes: Kristin became a nurse for burn patients.

© Tad Hardin

Tad's suitcase during Flight 1420.

Tad Hardin described his journey through survivor's guilt: "We came around to be grateful recipients of God's grace. Spared from a horrific death, God's purpose has been magnified in allowing us to worship Him and encounter the Holy Spirit." As Tad reflected on the recent 21-year anniversary, these lyrics resonate from a song his choir sang during their trip:

> Oh, let me hear Thee Speaking, In accents clear and still,
> Above the storms of passion, The murmurs of self-will;
> Oh, speak to reassure me, To hasten, or control;
> Oh, speak, and make me listen, Thou Guardian of my soul.

"Nothing earthly is secure. The only thing eternal is salvation through eternal life. Our faith can be refined, and strengthened, by seasons. Telling the story at first was hard, but I experienced a nudge from the Lord. Maybe telling my story is not just for me, but I can help others get unstuck."

A professor of piano studies at Liberty University, Tad Hardin has shared his story during several of our Aeronautics classes. With gentleness and humility, Tad exudes a quality of Spirit-led hope and encouragement for others who may have also experienced difficulty in life. Christ's eternal purpose for Tad and Kristin continues to be fulfilled. What's your eternal purpose?

Ephesians 3:11.This was according to the eternal purpose that he has realized in Christ Jesus our Lord.

 Connect: Draw near and listen to God. How is He speaking to you?

Grow: Discuss today's theme with your wingman. Do you know your eternal purpose? Have you ever been in a harrowing accident or near-death experience?

Live: Where will you go, what will you do, and whom will you serve? How will you live today?

Prayer: *(From Tad Hardin) Lord, thank You that Your purpose for my life is steadfast and unspoiled by my shortcomings or sufferings. Speak ever clearly that I may never ignore Your call to serve and connect with others. May my past trauma and present weaknesses become tools in Your hands that mature my witness and refine my faith. Amen.*

My response:

Connect

Grow

Live

Day 19

Listen and Believe

Romans 10:9. Because, if you confess with your mouth that Jesus is Lord and believe in your heart that God raised Him from the dead, you will be saved.

Life includes moments on the mountaintops and in the valleys. I was saved at a young age, but have lived through seasons where my faith in Jesus Christ seemed futile — even during my latter years walking closely with the Lord, engaging in daily devotions, attending and serving in ministry leadership roles, and doing what seemed to be all the right things. Sometimes God lets the boat rock so He can teach us it's not only His voyage, but His storm too.

I was deployed to Central America flying C-130 missions in America's war on drugs. My wife called, "Mitch, something's up, the baby's not moving like before, I don't feel right." Lord, protect my wife and fourth child, comfort her. There were days of anxiety before I came home to accompany her to the medical center. The doctor viewing the ultrasound shook his head: "I'm sorry, Commander." Tears filled our eyes and anguish gripped our broken hearts.

It's Not Only His Voyage, but His Storm Too

Less than a year later, we had the same difficult time when another baby was lost. Finally, our miracle baby came a few weeks before my wife's 40th birthday. After three boys, a girl! God took away my bitterness-induced frustration and turned it to hope-filled joy. He doesn't command faithfulness in order to give me His gift of salvation, however, He provides the strength and power I need to choose to honor His gift with more faith. Have you ever been at a point in your life where all hope is gone and there's no other choice but to listen, believe, and trust in Christ?

Psalm 37:3. Trust in the Lord, and do good; dwell in the land and befriend faithfulness.

Connect: Draw near and listen to God. How is He speaking to you?

Grow: Discuss today's theme with your wingman. How has God carried you during a "valley" life season?

Live: Where will you go, what will you do, and whom will you serve? How will you live today?

Prayer: Jesus, I couldn't make it in life's valleys without You by my side. Sometimes life is hard and I don't understand why difficult days come, even when it seems I'm in fellowship with You. But You, God, remain steadfast and faithful, providing me with treasures new and old every day. Your mercy, grace, and love provide a peace I can't explain. When frustrated and weak, Lord, I need to rely on You more. Whether crawling in valleys or climbing on mountaintops, God, let me praise You. Because I know You're here for me. Let the words of my mouth and the meditations of my heart be pleasing to You. In Your name I ask, Amen.

My response:

Connect

Grow

Live

Faith in Christ

John 14:6. Jesus said to him, I am the way, the truth, and the life. No one comes to the Father except through Me.

Trusting Jesus Christ remains the most important life decision I have ever made. More important that dropping to a knee to ask my wife to marry me, or the day I raised my right hand to serve in the military. But I'm going to be honest, having faith in Christ isn't a one and done kind of thing for me. It takes a lot of work—the hard kind, from the inside out. The toughest part is I can't fake it because God sees right through me. No, I don't keep getting saved over and over again. But now that I have my salvation, God asks me to work it out.

I'm His, Regardless of Airspeed or Rotor RPM

Airplane wings create lift, based on relative wind over the airfoil. When an airplane slows to a critical stall speed, one wing falls creating a spin, loss of altitude, and eventual ground contact. Helicopter rotors rotate at a minimum speed. Otherwise the blades cone, ceasing to bear the weight of the machine, which stops beating the air into submission. Flight aerodynamics remain finite and unchangeable. But God's steadfast provision for us defies human logic.

We all experience crash-and-burn moments. In many cases, God doesn't prevent the crash. I suspect that when I crash, it's part of His plan. But I'm His, regardless of airspeed or rotor RPM. Soaring over the highest mountaintop or scud running in the lowest valley, He remains with me. Because He never leaves or forsakes me, I can pick myself up and fly again.

Isaiah 53:5-6. But He was pierced for our transgressions; He was crushed for our iniquities; upon Him was the chastisement that brought us peace, and with His wounds we are healed. All we like sheep have gone astray; we have turned -every one- to his own way; and the Lord has laid on Him the iniquity of us all.

Connect: Draw near and listen to God. How is He speaking to you?

Grow: Discuss today's theme with your wingman. How's your airspeed or rotor RPM today? Encourage each other: God loves you no matter what.

Live: Where will you go, what will you do, and whom will you serve? How will you live today?

Prayer: *Dear God, You draw us to Your heart and lavish us with Your love, favor, and blessing. How amazing that You provided a perfect Lamb in Jesus who was crushed for my iniquity and pierced for my transgression. By His wounds and death, I am forgiven. He is risen and intercedes for me. You provide the power of Your Holy Spirit to work in my heart and life to change me from the inside out. Thank You that I don't have to perform to earn Your gift; I just need to have faith. Hallelujah, Father, that You pick me up daily and let me fly again. May I soar with Your joy and purpose! In Your precious name, I pray. Amen.*

My response:

Connect

Grow

Live

New Creation

2 Corinthians 5:17. Therefore, if anyone is in Christ, he is a new creation. The old has passed away; behold, the new has come.

"Sorry, Dad, I got a ticket for 91 in a 60 last night. I'll be at a friend's house. I'm okay and we'll talk later in the morning."

A stirring inside my soul calmed my fears. He'll be okay. Love, don't punish him. We had a "once a lifetime" talk on the drive home. I'll never forget the day our oldest son decided his purpose in life was to serve others, not himself.

A few weeks later, we met the judge to resolve the reckless driving charge. I thanked the officer for pulling my kid over that night: "Keep doing your job well. You're making a difference!" I don't know where we would be today had God not worked in both of us. The Lord changed the way I parented, from rules-based to values-based. And the Lord certainly transformed our son in a powerful, radical way. The sort of change that you can't help but marvel over — a miracle. Decades of prayers faithfully answered, in God's time.

One of my life's treasured moments was when I baptized our firstborn son. Many of us had prayed God's blessing upon him. Parents, grandparents, uncles, aunts, pastors, coaches, teachers, and friends. The outward expression of true, repentant faith in Jesus: "I baptize you in the name of the Father, Son, and Holy Spirit. Buried in death to self, raised to walk in newness of life."

Now, I'm dad for a growing shepherd currently serving as a ministry leader who loves, mentors, and encourages suburban-Atlanta middle and high school students with joy, passion, innovation, and creativity. He lives with wisdom, humility, and energy. This is my son, in whom I am well pleased!

Thank You, Lord. You taught me a valuable life lesson on how to love a prodigal son. Long ago, I was the son needing to find the way home. God, with open arms, steadfast love, and gentle forgiveness, You remain faithful. May I learn from your Father's heart!

Isaiah 43:19. Behold, I am doing a new thing; now it springs forth, do you not perceive it? I will make a way in the wilderness and rivers in the desert.

Connect: Draw near and listen to God. How is He speaking to you?

Grow: Discuss today's theme with your wingman. Have you ever felt like you were running away, from parents, from life, and from God?

Live: Where will you go, what will you do, and whom will you serve? How will you live today?

Prayer: (From Cam Morrison). Dear God, thank You for Your mercy. I thank You for all that You've done in my life because every step of it draws me closer to You. In the journey, You're right there beside me. Although I may drift away, I know that You're with me day by day. The same way a shepherd cares for his sheep, anoints their heads with oil, steers and directs such blind animals away from danger, so You have cared for me God. You found me, You called me Your own, and You made me a new creation. Help me walk as the new creation You have made me to be. I love You, Jesus. Amen.

My response:

Connect

Grow

Live

Believe and Abide

Genesis 15:6. Then he believed in the Lord and He counted it to him as righteousness.

Brigadier General Frank Savage took over the 918th Bomb Group when Colonel Keith Davenport had given his all. In *Twelve O'Clock High*, we learn about the early days of precision daylight bombing by a U.S. Army Air Forces B-17 bomber unit striving to defeat the Third Reich. I've used this film as a leadership and identity teaching platform for more than 25 years. Over 90% of my students rate the black and white film as a semester highlight.

Savage entered command with an expectation of professionalism, pride, and grit. He tells the airmen, "We're in a war, a shooting war, and we've gotta fight. And some of us have got to die." He tells his men they don't need to see the end (of going home) but just believe in their ability to make the grade now (22.1). The tension of conversations with senior leaders hinted at doubts of losing the war if the men's efforts failed. It was a tough job: U.S. bomber crew losses in Europe were among the highest of any World War II military profession.

Over time, the frazzled men gained confidence in their unit, their leaders, and themselves. Actor Dean Jagger played the character of Major Harvey Stovall, a lawyer turned non-flying air unit administrator. Jagger won the 1949 Academy Award for best supporting actor (22.2). Demoted and humiliated Lieutenant Colonel Ben Gately went from Davenport's second-in-command to only a line pilot role, leading the Group's deadbeats and misfits in a bomber dubbed "Leper Colony."

The 918th flight surgeon, Doc Kaiser, described Savage's breakdown as a "maximum effort." Brigadier General Frank Savage built the foundation for his unit to thrive and contribute to defeat Nazi Germany. When Savage folded, Gately willingly and courageously took the General's place to lead the Group. Have you ever given a maximum effort and folded in defeat, even when trusting God? I believe the Lord places us in life seasons of difficulty and trial to allow us to trust him more.

(22.1) *Twelve O'Clock High*: Produced by Darryl F. Zanuck, Twentieth Century Studios, 1949.

(22.2) Davis, B. (2017). Airman Magazine. Retrieved from https://airman.dodlive.mil/ 2017/11/06/bombs-away/

John 15:5. I am the vine; you are the branches. Whoever abides in Me and I in him, he it is that bears much fruit, for apart from Me you can do nothing.

 Connect: Draw near and listen to God. What do you sense today? How is He speaking to you?

Grow: Discuss today's theme with your wingman. Describe a time you worked to the point of exhaustion and perhaps failed. While it was difficult then, what did you learn?

Live: Where will you go, what will you do, and whom will you serve? How will you live today?

Prayer: Heavenly Father, thank You Lord for Your faithfulness and mercy. We're grateful to learn from stories about real heroes who fought through fear with courage and determination. Today, when we give our all and fail You, God, restore us with Your grace. Apart from You, Jesus, we can do nothing. Grant us more trust, more faith, and more grit to abide in You, and to support each other in the real fight today against evil forces in the spiritual realm. In the power of the Holy Spirit, we run toward the fight —in the classroom, on the flight decks, in our homes, wherever our job leads. We stand in the strong name of Jesus, our Christ! You promise us in the end we win the fight. In faith, Lord, we believe! Amen.

My response:

Connect

Grow

Live

Stand in Grace

Romans 5:1-2. Therefore, since we have been justified by faith, we have peace with God through our Lord Jesus Christ. Through Him we have also obtained access by faith into this grace in which we stand, and we rejoice in hope of the glory of God.

Pinnacle 4701 departed Little Rock, Arkansas October 14, 2004 en route to Minneapolis in a regional jet with no passengers on a repositioning flight. Five seconds after takeoff, the aircraft was pitched 22 degrees nose up for a rapid climb. The captain commented to air traffic control they didn't have passengers and "decided to have a little fun," climbing to FL410. Unable to sustain level flight at 41,000 feet mean sea level, both engines flamed out unexpectedly in a pilot-induced aerodynamic stall. Trying to restart, the distracted pilots crashed to their deaths two and a half miles short of the airport in Jefferson City, Missouri. The last words: "Aw #. . . we're gonna hit houses dude" (23.1). How could two professional airline pilots crash a multi-million dollar jet? Before condemning them, I need to consider what I've done.

Watch This!

The "D" model OH-58 was new and I was on a gunnery reconnaissance training mission with several Army attack and observation helicopters at a training range in West Germany. Confidence in my aircraft and flying ability got the best of me. I said to the Artillery Lieutenant in the left seat, "Watch this!" My friend Scott Burns came onto the intercom, "Whoa. . .. Ohhhh. . .. Ahhhh. . .. Wow!" A comment from one of the Cobras in the formation on Victor (pilot-speak for the radio frequency), "Showoff." Then nothing else. Not a post-brief comment. Never another mention, ever. Except in my conscience.

I had executed a 360-degree pedal turn in the middle of an eight aircraft flight while traveling over the range road at 40–50 knots. With the lead aircraft not keeping the speed up, and the frustration of being in the middle, having to speed up and slow down, I took advantage to slow down by flying sideways, then backwards, a full 360-degree pedal turn at 45 knots, then recovering. Not my most professional moment as an Army aviator. God gave me the choice to fix it on my own, without reprimand or sanction. I decided

(23.1) NTSB Report - Pinnacle 4701: https://ntsb.gov/investigations/AccidentReports/Reports/AAR0701.pdf

to never fly like a show-off again. Before condemning others, I need to look within to see my own flaws.

I'm grateful for lessons learned and grace received from God. Over time, I've learned to forgive myself when I fall short. With faith in Jesus, I have His forgiveness and look forward to glory.

Psalm 13:5. But I have trusted in Your loving kindness; my heart shall rejoice in Your salvation.

 Connect: Draw near and listen to God. How is He speaking to you?

Grow: Discuss today's theme with your wingman. Discuss what you can learn from others' mistakes. Do you need to change your behavior?

Live: Where will you go, what will you do, and whom will you serve? How will you live today?

Prayer: Lord, there is no one without sin or fault, except for Jesus. May we learn from the mistakes of others, and seek to do that which is good, right, and professional. May we fight the urge to say "Watch this!" For those of us who have messed up, let us learn and change our behavior for the sake of those we serve, our passengers, families, and colleagues. To the glory of God, Amen.

My response:

Connect

Grow

Live

Eternal Future

Isaiah 26:4. Trust in the Lord forever, for the Lord God is an everlasting rock.

American Airlines Captain Charles "Chic" Burlingame commanded one of four jets hijacked by Islamic terrorists on September 11, 2001. Chic's brother Brad received a phone call from a family friend, "Chic has been killed." The Burlingame brothers grew up near Anaheim stadium in Southern California and were huge Angels' fans, like me (24.1).

On the 10-year anniversary of the most historic day of the 21st century, *Orange County Register* reporter Eric Carpenter told Brad Burlingame's story of healing (24.2). His brother's aircraft, American Airlines Flight 77 crashed into the Pentagon, killing 64 people on board and another 125 on the ground (24.3). Full of jet fuel, the aircraft and part of the Pentagon building burned, leaving little remains. Recovery workers found the remnants of a burnt prayer card from the Burlingame brothers' mom's funeral Chic had carried.

＊ ＊ ＊

"I am the soft stars that shine at night. Do not stand at the grave and cry; I am not there, I did not die."

Mr. Carpenter wrote, says Brad: "It was my mom talking to us, saying, 'He's OK; he's with me now.'" Although Brad Burlingame died of cancer in 2015, his family's story serves as an inspiration of trust in the midst of tragedy.

On September 10, 2001, I served as the overnight Senior Duty Officer at Coast Guard Air Station Sacramento. I woke up to see the same horrific sights on TV that Brad Burlingame watched, forever seared into my memory. I don't know why that day occurred, but I trust God's purpose and plans. Our Heavenly Father uses all things for good, including Chic Burlingame's prayer card that survived the fiery crash at the Pentagon. I hope Jesus can introduce me to Chic and Brad in heaven.

Colossians 3:2. Set your mind on things that are above, not on things that are on earth.

(24.1) Flight and Faith Blog, Dr. Mitchell Morrison: June 28, 2019.

(24.2) Carpenter, E. September 11, 2011. *Orange County Register*.

(24.3) History Channel webpage. Retrieved from https://www.history.com/news/pentagon-design-september-11-attacks

Connect: Draw near and listen to God. How is He speaking to you?

Grow: Discuss today's theme with your wingman. Where were you (or your parents) on September 11, 2001? How did this fateful day impact you or those you love?

Live: Where will you go, what will you do, and whom will you serve? How will you live today?

Prayer: Dear Lord, Your purpose and plans sometimes are difficult to under-stand. But we rest and trust in Your heart and promise of heaven. Allow us to set our minds on Your things and see You as our everlasting rock. Thank You Father for the blessings of life, and for the memories of brave people who died on September 11, 2001. We ask for Your favor and strength for those who remain and wait for Your glory in Heaven. In Jesus' name, Amen.

My response:

Connect

Grow

Live

How to Live

Matthew 5:16. In the same way, let your light shine before others, so that they may see your good works and give glory to your Father who is in heaven.

Great aviation mentors shaped my early career learning. Some said, "Let me show you something I learned in Vietnam!" They told stories about near-fatal mistakes in combat and highlighted the importance of memorizing aircraft emergency procedures and limits. You need to know what the book says and when deviating is warranted for survival. The oldest and most experienced fought to generate unit camaraderie and loyalty. As the young new guy, I became a mascot, or protégé, but they never condemned or put me down. The best appeared to already know everything, but always strove to improve.

Know and Live by the Book

In addition to training missions and hangar flying, learning my craft as a helicopter pilot in the 1980s came through reading the technical publications. I discerned that if I wanted to stay alive in combat, I would need to know and fly by the book. I studied my flight manuals a lot.

These days, I need to study my life manual: The Bible. The same principle applies — if I want to stay alive in spiritual combat, I need to know and live by the book. Several years ago, I adopted a life verse: Micah 6:8. Do what's right, love people, and keep my ego in check. However, I'm beginning to enjoy Matthew 13:52: Treasure new and old. The treasure isn't physical or financial wealth. New treasure is God's continued work and blessing that unfolds before my eyes every day. Old treasure consists of memories experienced; knowledge learned; relationships with family and friends; and past events the Lord has woven together in the tapestry of my life.

What verse, memories, and learning guide you?

Micah 6:8. He has told you, O man, what is good; and what does the Lord require of you but to do justice, and to love kindness, and to walk humbly with your God.

Connect: Draw near and listen to God. How is He speaking to you?

Grow: Discuss today's theme with your wingman. Do you have a life verse?

Live: Where will you go, what will you do, and whom will you serve? How will you live today?

Prayer: Dear Heavenly Father, thank You for aviation mentors early in my career who I now realize truly loved me. They taught me how to protect myself in combat and in life. I need to know and fly by the book as a pilot. Lord, I also want to learn and live by the book as a follower of Jesus Christ. May You guide my heart as I continue to grow each day. No matter how much I know, it's not what I say, or write. It's only as good as things put into action, Lord, bearing the fruit of the Holy Spirit. May I do the right thing, love people, and never let ego (edging God out) to rule over me. I pray a special blessing upon mentors and friends You have blessed me with, and those You continue to bring into my life today. May I serve as one who truly loves others myself, giving back to the legacy of those who taught me well. In Jesus' name I pray, Amen.

My response:

Connect

Grow

Live

God's Bigger Plan

John 9:2-3. And His disciples asked Him, Rabbi, who sinned, this man or his parents, that he was born blind? Jesus answered, It was not that this man sinned, or his parents, but that the works of God might be displayed in him.

We heard a knock on the front glass at the Los Angeles Air Station entrance door. Located in the midst of the two sprawling dual-runway complexes at LAX, we had a fenced parking lot and a big hangar. My office was near the door but someone else had already noticed a group of people including a boy about eight years old. An older gentleman in the group looked familiar.

We were on a routine ready crew flight and heard a call on Channel 16 about an overdue boat towing a sailing vessel. A few minutes into the shoreline search, the rescue swimmer commented, "Sir, what's that down there?" "That's a boogie boarder!" I circled downward to notice a man with a red polo shirt, blue running shorts, and a gray beard clinging to a piece of wood. He waved feebly as the rotor wash pelted the chilly Pacific seawater.

Thanks for Finding Me!

We quickly got him on board and landed at the Torrance hospital helipad so quickly that the staff had little time to prepare for our arrival. The guy's core body temperature was 95.4°F and the doctors said he had only a few minutes to survive before succumbing too hypothermia.

The visitor that Wednesday before Thanksgiving was the same man. He smiled. "I just wanted to introduce you to my grandson. He's glad you found me that day. Thanks for finding me!" Years of training and preparation for things to line up for my rescue helicopter crew to be in the right place and time to make a difference. It wasn't dark or stormy, but equally perilous for that guy. We were sent out, and made a difference for that family. A lifetime spent studying in school, learning the basics, applying specialized training as a pilot. Culminating with five minutes so the works of God could be displayed.

Isaiah 6:8. And I heard the voice of the Lord saying, "Whom shall I send, and who will go for Us?" Then I said, "Here I am! Send me."

Connect: Draw near and listen to God. How is He speaking to you?

Grow: Discuss today's theme with your wingman. It may be years before you accomplish a fulfilling task in aviation, but it will come. Where do you plan to serve?

Live: Where will you go, what will you do, and whom will you serve? How will you live today?

Prayer: Lord, thank You for the opportunity to serve our country in the Coast Guard. What a blessing to be used to locate and rescue that towboat captain during his time of need! Thank You, Lord, for sending his family that day, and whose gratitude powerfully blessed us! In Jesus' name, Amen.

My response:

Connect

Grow

Live

Obey

Ezekiel 36:26. And I will give you a new heart, and a new spirit I will put within you. And I will remove the heart of stone from your flesh and give you a heart of flesh. And I will put my Spirit within you, and cause you to walk in my statutes and be careful to obey my rules.

As a four-year-old boy, I carried the ring down the aisle at the Anaheim church house during Larry and Pat Clements' wedding. Made of gold, this circle represented God's unbroken love and symbol of commitment and promise from a groom to his bride. In 1968, I had no clue what an honor it was to serve two people who in 2020 recently celebrated their 52nd anniversary.

One day in the parking lot of that church, I was playing with friends and called him a SOB under my breath. Pat's dad, the senior pastor and WW2 Army veteran, was passing by. He stared at me, shaking his head. Later, he lovingly challenged me. His deep, stern voice asked: "Do you cuss?" Iron sharpens iron. I needed to obey God more rather than falling prey to mischief with my peers. I chose looking "cool" by saying words heard from others, not knowing what they really meant. I understand now why parents and leaders correct children.

Little Steps of Obedience

I'm sharpened and challenged, too, by the lasting memory of Larry sitting in the living room of our La Palma house: Bible open, tears streaming, pleading with dad and mom to fight for their crumbling marriage that ended in divorce. It took years, even decades, but God has been steadfast and faithful to turn a mess into a message. Good news: Mom and dad have lovingly forgiven each other, an example of restoration and healing as they walk with the Lord. No doubt, they too, and many others have been blessed by Larry and Pat's obedient legacy. All to the glory of God!

© *Larry Clements*

Pat Clements wearing her wedding ring, May 2020.

1 Timothy 1:5. The aim of our charge is love that issues from a pure heart and a good conscience and a sincere faith.

 Connect: Draw near and listen to God. How is He speaking to you?

Grow: Discuss today's theme with your wingman. Who has been an example or offered encouragement? When needed, who has challenged you to obey? Who do you need to forgive or restore?

Live: Where will you go, what will you do, and whom will you serve? How will you live today?

Prayer: (From Pastor Mark Clements, Larry and Pat's son) Heavenly Father, thank You for the gift of marriage. Thank You for the never-ending, unfailing love of Jesus for His bride, which marriage represents. Remind us that every broken relationship that is restored by Christ's love and forgiveness shouts the Gospel of Jesus for all the world to see. Thank You for people like my parents, who display the covenant-keeping love of Christ every day they choose to honor their covenant of marriage. Give us the courage to obey You in every circumstance, not based on emotions, but motivated by the covenant You have made with us. In Jesus' name, Amen.

My response:

Connect

Grow

Live

Get Right with Him

1 John 1:9. If we confess our sins, he is faithful and just to forgive us our sins and to cleanse us from all unrighteousness.

At 11:38 a.m. Eastern Standard Time on January 28, 1986, NASA's Space Shuttle program appeared near the pinnacle of achievement. Christa McAuliffe was added in July 1975 to join the crew as America's first teacher in space. Public interest hadn't been stronger since Neil Armstrong's 1969 lunar walk. Researchers readied the Spartan Satellite for deployment to observe Halley's Comet, an event occurring only once every 76 years (28.1).

Yield from Pride and Ego

I remember seeing Halley's Comet in 1986 through the tubes of old-school ANVIS-5 night vision goggles on an early morning OH-58 training mission in Dona Ana Range. The comet appeared low on the horizon, shining bright and clear like a sparkling fireball shot from a medieval catapult. Another memory during that season: I was at the hangar when a colleague said Challenger blew up after takeoff from Cape Canaveral. We had seen the shuttle piggy-backed on a massive Boeing 747. The craft had stopped at our base at Biggs Army Airfield while en route to Florida from landing at Edwards Air Force Base in California.

President Reagan chartered an independent review led by former U.S. Attorney General and Secretary of State William P. Rogers. The team's vice chairman was moon mission hero Neil Armstrong and included the first man to fly at Mach 1.0, Chuck Yeager. Rogers' team reported safety concerns: "A serious flaw in the decision making process." In NASA's mid-1980s culture, senior leaders ridiculed mid-level engineers for dissent and required proof equipment was *unsafe* rather than safe. In case you're wondering, that's backwards.

The STS 51-L launch proceeded despite freezing weather. Rubber joints in the massive fuel tanks leaked, causing the catastrophic explosion at approximately 46,000 feet while traveling at near twice the speed of sound. I use the heartbreaking Challenger case to teach students the importance of honest communications and reporting of safety information.

(28.1) NASA website. Retrieved from https://spaceflight.nasa.gov/outreach/SignificantIncidents/assets/rogers_commission_report.pdf

We must yield from pride and ego to properly mitigate risks and control hazards. But it's more than just a safety decision. We need to trust in God to guide our thinking.

Psalm 51:10. Create in me a clean heart, O God, and renew a right spirit within me.

 Connect: Draw near and listen to God. How is He speaking to you?

Grow: Discuss today's theme with your wingman. Have you ever wanted to press on with something, even though someone cautioned you?

Live: Where will you go, what will you do, and whom will you serve? How will you live today?

Prayer: Lord, we don't throw stones at those who decided to launch Space Shuttle Challenger, because we've all failed too. We honor the legacy of the brave astronauts who died that day. Would You allow us to learn from this tragedy, and listen when others speak up? Give us Your wisdom to build the right culture in our lives, with our family and church, in the office, on our flight decks, and in the shadows of our private personal areas. God, shine Your light in the darkness. We want to get our hearts right with You. In Jesus' name, Amen.

My response:

Connect

Grow

Live

True with God

Romans 12:2. Do not be conformed to this world, but be transformed by the renewal of your mind, that by testing you may discern what is the will of God, what is good and acceptable and perfect.

Fourteen-year-old Abrahamek Koplowicz wanted to fly, but the teen never reached his goal. Koplowicz was murdered in 1943 by the Nazis in Auschwitz, but his journal was found in an attic. The words live on today, displayed at Jerusalem's Yad Vashem Holocaust Museum:

> *When I grow up and get to be twenty I'll travel and see this world of plenty.*
>
> *In a bird with an engine I will sit myself down, Take off and fly into space, far above the ground.*
>
> *I'll fly, I'll cruise and soar up high Above a world so lovely, into the sky.*

Abrahamek's poem encourages me to practice three lifelong learning tenets with action, focus, and intentionality: 1) be grateful; 2) fail forward and 3) remain present today. The Jewish boy couldn't realize his dream of flight, but I can tell his story to inspire someone else. Even after many years, the joy and fun of flight makes me smile. With privilege and opportunity to serve in aviation, let me remember the anticipation and excitement written by a teen killed in a German concentration camp. May I practice "gratitude," "fail forward," and "remain present" today (29.1).

Habakkuk 3:18. Yet I will rejoice in the Lord; I will take joy in the God of my salvation.

(29.1) Adapted from Flight and Faith blog, Dr. Mitchell Morrison: July 8, 2019.

Connect: Draw near and listen to God. How is He speaking to you?

Grow: Discuss today's theme with your wingman. What can you do today to express gratitude, fail forward, and be present and mindful?

Live: Where will you go, what will you do, and whom will you serve? How will you live today?

Prayer: Thank You God for giving me the opportunity to make my life matter. May we never become so burdened and distracted that we lose sight of the precious gifts You provide each day. Give us the precious excitement of a young, aspiring heart, like this Jewish teen whose life was taken too soon. Transform us, Lord, renew our minds so we can turn away from fear of failing and move forward. Give us discernment of delight and excitement for Your calling and purpose upon our lives. May we rejoice in the joy of Your salvation today on earth. We ask in Jesus' name, Amen.

My response:

Connect

Grow

Live

God on Throne, Not Me

Psalm 139:23. Search me, O God, and know my heart! Try me and know my thoughts.

Military spouses bear an emotional burden of saying goodbye to their husbands or wives during operations, training, and conflict. I know a military pilot who served in three major combat operations and spent several years separated from his wife and children while serving his country. Although he could easily dwell on his service and actions over those wartorn years, he continues to express utmost admiration and sincere gratitude for the steadfast dedication, sacrifice, and service of his wife and family.

During my own retirement ceremony from the Coast Guard, a highlight for me was to acknowledge the sacrifice and commitment by my own wife and kids who trusted God when I was away standing the watch. Many life stories were written and family work accomplished during my thousands of hours in flight and several days, weeks, and months spent on duty. They carry on without us: Strong warriors and brave heroes receiving little recognition.

True and Faithful

As I think about my life as a pilot, I flew many exciting missions but I also remember fond moments of returning home. True and faithful loved ones are a gift from God! May we never take them for granted.

1 Corinthians 10:5. We destroy arguments and every lofty opinion raised against the knowledge of God, and take every thought captive to obey Christ.

Connect: Draw near and listen to God. How is He speaking to you?

Grow: Discuss today's theme with your wingman. How do you plan to handle time apart from those you love?

Live: Where will you go, what will you do, and whom will you serve? How will you live today?

Prayer: Lord, thank You for loving, hard-working wives and husbands who support their loved ones flying, maintaining, and supporting aviation operations all over the world be it airlines, military, mission and humanitarian organizations, corporate flying, or in general aviation, You have called us to serve with professionalism and dedication. Protect and guide us as we remain true and faithful. Allow us remember the sacrifice and love of those who wait for us to come home. We remain grateful for their brave support and warriors heart as they carry on faithfully without us physically, but remain present in heart and spirit. With the equipping power and strength of Your Holy Spirit, God, we dedicate ourselves to serve them well. We ask in Jesus' name, Amen.

My response:

Connect

Grow

Live

Choose Now

Joshua 24:15. And if it is evil in your eyes to serve the Lord, choose this day whom you will serve, whether the gods your fathers served in the region beyond the River, or the gods of the Amorites in whose land you dwell. But as for me and my house, we will serve the Lord.

I was at a mid-90's Promise Keepers rally in the Los Angeles Coliseum with 70,000 other men. A worship leader encouraged us: "As trees planted by living water, come on men, lift up your branches to the Lord!" Raised in a conservative Baptist church, I was quiet and reserved. That night I raised my hands in worship for the first time. Later the same evening a pastor encouraged racial unity, reconciliation, and forgiveness. I connected with a similar-aged black man briefly. We embraced as brothers in Christ, telling each other: "No more!" God was calling me to lead others, but couldn't work through me until working in me.

Trophy of His Grace

As I continued in prayer for wisdom about next steps, I sensed God inviting me into a season to grow. It's one thing to raise my hands and embrace a brother during a worship service, but it became real when I trusted a Christian counselor to confront old wounds. The biggest was how I handled conflict: I felt cornered, condemned, and put down. Sometimes, I acted out with anger and defensiveness to prove myself right. The Lord changed my life, helping me grow out of ego-filled arrogance, unjust stigma, hateful shame, and spiteful condemnation. God led me to forgive myself and others which brought a sense of peace and closure. I gave my dad a framed letter to honor and thank him and shared my story at a men's retreat about tribute and blessing. God used my testimony as a trophy of His grace. With Him, I don't have to be right every time.

God has placed in us a story others can learn from. What's yours?

Philippians 4:8. Finally, brothers, whatever is true, whatever is honorable, whatever is just, whatever is pure, whatever is lovely, whatever is commendable, if there is any excellence, if there is anything worthy of praise, think about these things.

Connect: Draw near and listen to God. How is He speaking to you?

Grow: Discuss today's theme with your wingman. How are you doing, really?

Live: Where will you go, what will you do, and whom will you serve? How will you live today?

Prayer: *Lord, thank You for Your grace in letting me see how my ego got in the way of Your work through me. You don't want me to think less of myself because I'm Yours. However, may I always think of myself less by serving and leading others. May I relate with them in Your gentleness and grace even if I think I'm right. As for me and my house, Lord, please continue to empower and equip me and my family. We seek to serve and honor You with an eternal perspective. I ask in Jesus' name, Amen.*

My response:

Connect

Grow

Live

Be Strong

Ephesians 6:10-11. Finally, be strong in the Lord and in the strength of His might. Put on the whole armor of God, that you may be able to stand against the schemes of the devil.

You met Jim Crismon on Day 3. Let's go to rural Arkansas in 1966 and view the setting from Jim's eyes in a letter he wrote to me personally. This is excerpted by permission from my book, *Teamworks* (32.1).

I had just accepted the job as Administrator of the hospital immediately after retiring from the Navy and preparing the hospital for Medicare funds was just part of the job. In 1966, Medicare had recently been enacted. When I went to the hospital it was still segregated but had received notice that there was to be an inspection by the Arkansas Board of Health to determine if the hospital qualified to receive Medicare funds. There were still segregated waiting rooms, rest rooms, drinking fountains and patient rooms with "White Only" and "Black Only" signs posted. I ordered the signs taken down and advised the staff that the hospital was totally integrated. I was making rounds of the hospital with the chief nurse and we came to a screened in porch that contained 3 or 4 hospital beds. It was June and HOT and the porch was not air-conditioned, yet there was one patient, a black man, out there. I asked the nurse if we had a room in the air-conditioned portion of the hospital where we could put the patient. She informed me that all rooms were occupied, so I asked if there was a two or three bed room with a vacant bed. She said there was one vacant bed in a two-bed room but that the President of the Board of Directors of the Hospital occupied the other bed. I pondered the situation and decided it was my job to integrate the hospital so might as well start now. I ordered the black man patient to be put in the empty bed in the room with the President of the Board. The nurse was stunned but she complied. I anticipated that my first day on the job would be my last one but never heard a word from anyone about "the integration." We passed the Medicare inspection and started receiving Medicare funds. There was never any opposition from anyone, nor any agency to the total integration of the hospital.

Reading this story, you see why I admired Master Chief Crismon so much. Doing the right thing sometimes has a cost. We may need to go against perception, political correctness, or tradition. Standing on the truth of scripture, prayer, and civility, we must root out the remnants of hateful treatment of

(32.1) Morrison, M. (2013). *Teamworks: Transforming Healthcare's Error-Prone Culture.* San Diego: Creative Team Publishing.

others because of their skin color! It begins with me: How I parent and lead my own children and how I teach and guide students and clients I encounter.

1 Samuel 12:20. And Samuel said to the people, "Do not be afraid; you have done all this evil. Yet do not turn aside from following the Lord, but serve the Lord with all your heart."

Connect: Draw near and listen to God. How is He speaking to you?

Grow: Discuss today's theme with your wingman. Pray about how God is calling you to respond to injustice.

Live: Where will you go, what will you do, and whom will you serve? How will you live today?

Prayer: *Heavenly Father, our nation has been rocked recently by protests and discourse over the unjust death of George Floyd, a 46-year-old black man who died at the hand of a white police officer in Minneapolis. Would You help all of us understand our part in bringing forth healing? Equip us with Your wisdom and grace, transform our thoughts to Your righteousness. Give us Your power to deny the forces of evil seeking to use freedom of speech and protest for hate and violence. Break the chains, Lord! Restore our nation toward Your heart, O God, in You we trust! In Jesus' name, Amen.*

My response:

Connect

Grow

Live

In the Fight

Psalm 19:14. Let the words of my mouth and the meditation of my heart be acceptable in Your sight, O Lord, my rock and my redeemer.

Early in my Coast Guard career, I served on a three-month helicopter deployment with a cutter patrol. We sailed from Oakland to Alaska, then Hawaii, Midway, Wake, Micronesia, Guam, and back. As we approached a sandy palm-swept atoll, men in small powered boats and ocean canoes met us with carved coconuts and other items. I leaned over the rail to talk with a teen in a canoe wearing only a dirty tattered beach towel as a skirt. I asked him to wait and went to our stateroom to retrieve a pair of jeans and skivvies. He gave me a huge conch shell and a toothy smile.

Our Captain dropped anchor and invited interested crew to go ashore. As I walked among the crude huts and wood shacks, I noticed the simplicity in which these people lived. A covered large common space with open walls stood prominent in the village center. I passed through, noticing the corpsman set up in an impromptu clinic to treat islanders. A small boy squirmed and cried in his mom's arms as doc worked on a nasty wound on his forehead. A handful of families with children waited patiently.

Source: Mitchell Morrison

Gratitude and Humility

Later I returned to the village center to see the same youngster with a huge smile on his face eating an ice cream cone. I pointed to him, smiled, and gestured to his mom who said, "It's the first time he's had this." Wearing only underwear and a glisten of melting vanilla running down his face and chest, the sight of the youngster gave me a life treasure. Electricity, air-conditioning, quality healthcare, and abundant food (including dozens of ice cream flavors) remain things I take for granted.

The enemy wants me distracted and complaining, but I need to fight. My life needs to reflect gratitude and humility not entitlement or arrogance. Thank You, Lord, for the wise Captain who stopped at that island for a memory of a lifetime.

Ephesians 6:12. For we do not wrestle against flesh and blood, but against the rulers, against the authorities, against the cosmic powers over this present darkness, against the spiritual forces of evil in the heavenly places.

 Connect: Draw near and listen to God. How is He speaking to you?

Grow: Discuss today's theme with your wingman. What do you take for granted?

Live: Where will you go, what will you do, and whom will you serve? How will you live today?

Prayer: Dear God, I don't know how You've led in that man's life who now is 30 years old, or more. As I teach others about leadership and service may You use this experience in me to Your glory. Empower me to fight the devil and live content rather than complaining. The smile of a kid eating an ice cream cone gave me a life treasure! Thank You, Father for the blessing to see the atolls of Micronesia. In Jesus' name, Amen.

My response:

Connect

Grow

Live

Wingman: Better Together

Ecclesiastes 4:9. Two are better than one, because they have a good reward for their toil. For if they fall, one will lift up his fellow. But woe to him who is alone when he falls and has not another to lift him up!

Scott Hinton and I had both recently completed basic training and arrived at the 60th Company WOC barracks at Fort Rucker, Alabama. At 18 years old, Scott was the youngest Warrant Officer Candidate I ever met during Army flight training. Hinton was exactly (yes, to the day) one year younger than me, and two weeks ahead, wearing a Navy Blue cap. Mine was red. We both graduated with our original class.

As I entered the room for Coast Guard Direct Commission Officer training in Yorktown, Virginia, I sat in the second row on the right side of the room. I noticed a familiar face in the front row: Scott Hinton. We became stick buddies during Dolphin helicopter transition training and eventually had an opportunity to fly together. Later in our careers, Scott and I also flew a C-130 together. I don't know how many Coast Guard aviators have a similar wingman legacies.

✳ ✳ ✳

One of my favorite stories from Hinton is the day he bailed out of an experimental airplane at low altitude when a wing fitting failed. A couple weeks earlier, Scott started a cross-country trip from North Carolina to Florida, but remembered the parachute sitting on his bedroom floor. He turned around, and went home to complete the trip another day, this time wearing the chute. That decision saved his life.

Having served together in the Army, Coast Guard, and collegiate aviation, Scott and I pick up where we left off. Even after months, we'd reconnect. Among God's most cherished blessings are friends who stick closer than a brother and sharpen me like iron, like Scott. Who can you call today and encourage?

1 Peter 4:10. As each has received a gift, use it to serve one another, as good stewards of God's varied grace.

Connect: Draw near and listen to God. How is He speaking to you?

Grow: Discuss today's theme with your wingman. Thank him/her for encouraging you and reflect on how you both can continue your friendship beyond the current setting.

Live: Where will you go, what will you do, and whom will you serve? How will you live today?

Prayer: (From Scott Hinton) Father, I recognize we all need a wingman. No fighter pilot patrols alone, and neither should I. The enemy is strong, and alone I am weak, but with You, I can do anything. Lord, give me the strength to sharpen iron and the gentleness to comfort. Protect me as we grow Your kingdom and fight in Your name. Let me be a wingman, as You are to me, and share a love for my brother that honors You. Lord, You love me completely as I am, without end. Thank You for always being with me, because with You I never fly solo. In Jesus' name, Amen.

My response:

Connect

Grow

Live

Serve Others

Philippians 2:3-4. Do nothing from selfish ambition or conceit, but in humility count others more significant than yourselves. Let each of you look not only to his own interests, but also to the interests of others.

God places us in circumstances to honor Him and bless others, not ourselves. Hurricane Katrina struck the U.S. Gulf Coast in 2005. Category 5 winds battered shorelines, devastated buildings, flooded homes, hurled debris, and breached levies. Thousands of families were stranded without food, medicine, and other basic needs creating one of the greatest Search and Rescue efforts in history. Empowered with three abiding core values — honor, respect, and devotion to duty — Coast Guard aviation sprung into action.

We Had Faith in Each Other

Rescue swimmers wielded axes and saws to cut into roofs, fighting angry people they had to leave behind (35.1). *Author's note: Check out the stories in the story from National Public Radio.* Using helicopters, pilots, and crews from more than a dozen Air Stations from as far away as Cape Cod and the West Coast, aviators rescued more than 33,000 people. On day five, President George W. Bush visited the Coast Guard air station in Mobile, Alabama. FEMA Director Mike Brown told Commanding Officer Dave Callahan the brief was "his" less than an hour prior to Air Force One landing. Callahan found a rescue swimmer who had just returned from the fray and placed him on camera for a few moments to tell the real story of Coast Guard heroism. The brief went live globally.

Coast Guard crews who had never worked together came together to bring forth a miracle. How? They walked and worked together in one accord. Many worked without electrical power and basic comforts. Callahan recalled the scene of an aircrew landing after a long mission, then walking up to a seasoned pilot who said, "Give me second, sir," and vomited (35.2). The reality sunk in—this is a real disaster! But everyone pitched in, rolled up their sleeves, and got the job done. As I write today's words, we're in the 40th day of the season of coronavirus. I see

(35.1) *National Public Radio (NPR)*, September 9, 2005. Retrieved from https://www.npr.org/templates/story/story.php?storyId=4838677

(35.2) Interview with RADM David Callahan, USCG (retired).

a theme of thanks for our responders and healthcare professionals, along with encouragement for resilience and hope. May God bless them all.

Zechariah 7:9-10. Thus says the Lord of hosts, render true judgments, show kindness and mercy to one another, do not oppress the widow, the fatherless, the sojourner, or the poor, and let none of you devise evil against another in your heart.

 Connect: Draw near and listen to God. How is He speaking to you?

Grow: Discuss today's theme with your wingman. Do you remember the hurricane Katrina season? What about COVID-19? How did you respond? What did you learn?

Live: Where will you go, what will you do, and whom will you serve? How will you live today?

Prayer: Heavenly Father, some of us experience that one moment during our life when we see it's truly real. It may be difficulty, victory, joy, defeat, but Lord, You give us others to work with and opportunities to make a difference. May we be faithful with Your gift. In Jesus' name, Amen.

My response:

Connect

Grow

Live

Waiting to Conquer

Revelation 21:6-7. And He said to me, It is done! I am the Alpha and the Omega, the beginning and the end. To the thirsty I will give from the spring of the water of life without payment. The one who conquers will have this heritage, and I will be his God and he will be my son.

On April 28, 2020, Mincaye of the Waodani went to be with the Lord. From Steve Saint's obituary posted on Facebook: "I have known Mincaye since I was a little boy when he took me under his wing and had his sons teach me to blowgun hunt. He was one of my dearest friends in the world. Yes, he killed my father, but he loved me and my family. One of my grandsons is named Mincaye" (36.1).

In 1956, a Piper aircraft piloted by missionary Nate Saint landed on a river sandbar in Ecuador. Saint, Jim Elliot, Pete Fleming, Ed McCully, and Roger Youdarian: Five men reaching out for Christ to the Waodani tribesmen lost their lives at the hand of Mincaye's and others' spears (36.2). But God used their story for good. Saint's widow continued to pray for the tribe along with Elliot's, and God opened a door for Elisabeth Elliot and Nate's sister Rachel to live with the Waodani (36.3). Through God's grace, Mincaye received Christ, and eventually Steve Saint too went to live on that river in Ecuador with his aunt.

In *End of the Spear* (36.4), Mincaye described his grandfathers' anger turning to love. In Steve's words, "This is something you can't explain in fiction, you have to live it to understand." You may know the story or have seen the movie.

My friend Jim Molloy and his wife Kelly visited Mincaye and his wife Ompodae earlier this year, sitting in their house for about an hour. Jim described Mincaye: "He sat us down and started talking nonstop, telling his story in the Way language with great energy and animation. We didn't understand the words, but we experienced his message of love and restoration" (36.5).

(36.1) Facebook post from ITEC, Steve Saint (April 29, 2020). Facebook post from ITEC.

(36.2) The great omission, Steve Saint (2001). The great omission. YWAM Publishing.

(36.3) Steve Saint. A Great Homecoming. Retrieved from https://www.youtube.com/watch?v=LAbS_2mWHPE&feature=youtube

(36.4) Testimony End of the Spear. Retrieved from https://www.youtube.com/watch? v=6AnomA1dyQI

(36.5) Interview with Jim Molloy

The Saint family oversees ITEC, a ministry organization that trains and equips others around the world for the Great Commission. ITEC Ecuador is a self-sustaining business that uses aviation to support ministry to people living in the jungle. They build Vans RV10 aircraft, and they operate commercial air service to jungle villages. Jim and Kelly visited Mincaye while working with ITEC Ecuador, who also hosts Wao vision trips to learn more about people living in the jungle.

Job 19:25-26. For I know that my Redeemer lives, and at the last He will stand upon the earth. And after my skin has been thus destroyed, yet in my flesh I shall see God.

 Connect: Draw near and listen to God. How is He speaking to you?

Grow: Discuss today's theme with your wingman. What do you think about Steve Saint and Mincaye's story?

Live: Where will you go, what will you do, and whom will you serve? How will you live today?

Prayer: *(From Jim Molloy) Father, we know that all things work together for good for those who love You and are called according to Your purpose. You are God, who can change the hearts of those who don't know You and those who oppose You. Please use us as Your instruments to make disciples through the teaching of Your word to those who don't know You as Lord and Savior. Allow us to love them with Your love. Amen.*

My response:

Connect

Grow

Live

He Will Finish

Philippians 1:6. And I am sure of this, that he who began a good work in you will bring it to completion at the day of Jesus Christ.

While driving to a volunteer event for my daughter's soccer team and listening to the morning church service on the radio, I received a text: *Pray for Ernie Rogers. He collapsed at church this morning.* I clasped my hand to my bride's and we lifted urgent prayers to the Lord. Ten minutes later, Pastor Jonathan Falwell announced: Ernie had collapsed at Thomas Road Baptist Church. A nearby responder used a defibrillator and started cardiopulmonary resuscitation. A few weeks later, I met with Mr. Rogers to hear his story (37.1).

"I was feeling fine and talking with friends. Upon finishing the conversation, I started to walk away and immediately collapsed. My friends later told me I said I was feeling dizzy right before collapsing. I do not remember saying anything. I had no out-of-body experience or appearance of angels. Nothing. The next thing I saw four hours later was my wife Terrye's face at the hospital emergency room and a team of people working all around me."

Ernie had experienced a ventricular tachycardia. His heart stopped, and the responder saved his life, breaking the T12 vertebrae and bruising several ribs in the process. God wasn't ready to call one of Liberty University's Aeronautics School founders home yet. According to Ernie, the experience has brought him closer to his wife and family. He has renewed energy and interest to continue serving as his church disaster response coordinator. He wants to finish strong.

During Rogers' time as a professor, he taught seven imperatives:

1. Education opens doors
2. Respect everyone
3. Be dependable and visible
4. Quick to listen and slow to speak
5. Don't make big things out of little things
6. Be real
7. Life is a marathon not a sprint

(37.1) Conversation with Captain J. Ernie Rogers, U.S. Navy (retired), co-founder of Liberty University School of Aeronautics.

Psalm 91:16. With long life I will satisfy him and show him my salvation.

 Connect: Draw near and listen to God. How is He speaking to you?

Grow: Discuss today's theme with your wingman. What would you think and say if you woke up looking at your closest friend from a hospital bed?

Live: Where will you go, what will you do, and whom will you serve? How will you live today?

Prayer: *(From Ernie Rogers) - Our Father God as I look out over Your beautiful creation of the Blue Ridge Mountains I marvel at Your works in the Beginning. You were there then, and You are here now! I know You have a plan for my life, please reveal Your plan to me as I study Your Torah given to Moses. Bless our country and give me the strength to stand up for Your way in the midst of sin and evil. I pray in the precious name of Your Son Jesus, Amen.*

Isaiah 40:31. But those who hope in the Lord will renew their strength. They will soar on wings like eagles; they will run and not grow weary, they will walk and not be faint.

My response:

Connect

Grow

Live

We Have Hope!

1 Thessalonians 4:13. But we do not want you to be uninformed, brothers, about those who are asleep, that you may not grieve as others do who have no hope.

My cell phone rang: "Sir, it's DC2, we have a report of a plane crash by Anacapa, it's a MD."—"I'm in Cerritos, please launch or divert the ready"—"Already done, sir."—"Okay, I'll be on my way in." As Assistant Operations Officer, I was taking Ops calls when my boss was out. Upon arrival, our Air Station facilities technician (Damage Controlman Petty Officer Second Class) standing the watch briefed me that two of our three helicopters were airborne. We assessed availability to continue search and rescue efforts, which soon turned to post-crash recovery for Alaska 261 and grim reality that 83 passengers and five crew members had lost their lives.

The MD-80 experienced an uncontrolled dive into the Pacific Ocean when the horizontal stabilizer trim system jackscrew assembly failed due to insufficient lubrication. Contributing to the accident included the airline's extended service interval and inadequate FAA program oversight (38.1). Knowing what happened doesn't bring loved ones back, but can serve to inform and prevent the next occurrence. Others need not bear the hurt and grief of a similar tragedy.

Promise of a Hope

The next morning, I commanded a first-light early morning search for survivors. We had already expended several sorties and saw little except a jet fuel sheen and small remnants of shattered wreckage. For me and three others on our crew, we had a chilling sense of life's frailty. I said a silent prayer for the crash victims' families that morning. When losing people we love, we hurt. But we grieve with the promise of a hope to see loved ones again who are in Christ.

Psalm 49:15. But God will ransom my soul from the power of Sheol, for He will receive me.

(38.1) NTSB Report. Retrieved from https://www.ntsb.gov/investigations/AccidentReports/Reports/AAR0201.pdf

Connect: Draw near and listen to God. How is He speaking to you?

Grow: Discuss today's theme with your wingman. Have you had to endure tragedy? What can we learn from the Alaska 261 case?

Live: Where will you go, what will you do, and whom will you serve? How will you live today?

Prayer: Lord, draw near to us, when we suffer with a broken heart due to unexpected things happening. You don't expect us not to hurt, because You tell us in Your word that You are near to the broken-hearted. When difficult circumstances come, Lord, we have the hope of Jesus Christ to carry us through tragedy. May the peace that passes all understanding come upon us. Father, shine Your face upon Your children. We look forward to the day when we reunite in heaven with those who are in Christ. We pray in Jesus' holy name. Amen.

My response:

Connect

Grow

Live

Temporal (Not Eternal) Death

John 14:3. And if I go and prepare a place for you, I will come again and will take you to Myself, that where I am you may be also.

Ten years ago, I traveled on a well-appointed command and control jet with Coast Guard colleagues to visit several families whose loved ones died in a tragic night midair collision over the sea between a C-130 rescue airplane and a military combat helicopter. Stopping in the U.S. Northeast, we went to one warm family's home that connected with me deeply.

Our briefing team included an Admiral, his wife, an aide, Chaplain, and myself. During our meeting, the young crewman's family told us about their son and brother whom they had loved. We ate cake, laughed, and cried with them. A few years later, the mom reached out to me, asking to receive a recording of her son's voice. The data was protected by the military investigation process, but over the course of several months, I worked through the steps and gained approval to grant the request.

We May Die, but We're Not Gone Forever

At the conclusion of our meeting, I hugged and thanked the mom for her patience, grace, and empathy. My arms around her, I felt God's presence, as if I was hugging her for their son. Few times in my life have events touched my soul like losing seven shipmates on Coast Guard Rescue 1705 and two brave Marines. But God's plans and destiny are not only about our temporal earthly life. We may die, but we're not gone forever. With Jesus, we have an eternal home and future with God in paradise. Before Moses died, he gave a blessing to each of the 12 tribes of Israel, including Jeshurun: "There is none like God, O Jeshurun, who rides through the heavens to your help, through the skies in His majesty. The eternal God is your dwelling place" (Deuteronomy 33:26-27a). During your time on earth, receive His Majesty's blessing of redeeming life in Christ.

Psalm 31:5. Into Your hand I commit my spirit; You have redeemed me, O Lord, faithful God.

Connect: Draw near and listen to God. How is He speaking to you?

Grow: Discuss today's theme with your wingman. Do you connect with the idea you are created for eternal purpose? How can you make life matter now?

Live: Where will you go, what will you do, whom will you serve? How will you live today?

Prayer: Heavenly Father, I abide in Your eternal presence as my dwelling place. Thank You, Lord for Your promise of redemption; and in Christ, build our faith for more than only a temporal life on earth. Prepare a place for us, and we look to You to provide us with grace today and hope for tomorrow. To Your honor and glory, I'm grateful to have served in the military. For those families who lost those they loved, would You grant the peace and comfort that only You can provide, Lord. In Jesus' name, Amen.

My response:

Connect

Grow

Live

Delivered

Daniel 12:1b-2. But at that time your people shall be delivered, everyone whose name shall be found written the book. And many of those who sleep in the dust of the earth shall awake, some to everlasting life, and some to shame and everlasting contempt.

In the John Gospel account of Christ's crucifixion, Jesus said "It is finished!" And He bowed His head and gave up His spirit. But that's not the end of the story. God resurrected Him, and hundreds saw Him as He imparted the Spirit upon His disciples and gloriously rose to Heaven. Paul wrote in Ephesians 1:19 about His surpassing power for those who believe.

A Real Hope That I Share

I had another theme planned for this segment, but a compelling story emerged less than three weeks ago. Missionary Joyce Lin went to be with the Lord on May 12, 2020 when her Kodiak airplane delivering COVID-19 test kits and school supplies went down two minutes after takeoff from Sentana, in New Guinea. Forty-year-old Lin served with Missionary Aviation Fellowship and a few days prior to her death wrote, "It may sound strange, but these trying times have enhanced my feeling of purpose here in Papua" (40.1). The last fatal MAF crash was 23 years ago.

Joyce's MAF teammate Brock Larson told about Lin's love for those she served: "The presence of God has given [the Papuan] people hope, a real hope that I share" (40.1). Lin's home church in Maryland shared heartfelt testimony of personal impact upon families in their congregation. MAF shared a video including Joyce's own story about becoming a missionary pilot that you can find on their webpage below. A team of investigators is reviewing the accident. Pray for Joyce's family and MAF colleagues, along with the people of Indonesia.

Romans 10:10-13. For with the heart one believes and is justified, and with the mouth one confesses and is saved. For the Scripture says, Everyone who believes in Him will not be put to shame. For there is no distinction between Jew and Greek; for the same Lord is Lord of all, bestowing His riches on all who call on Him. For everyone who calls on the name of the Lore will be saved.

(40.1) Burgess, C. Mission Aviation Fellowship webpage. Retrieved from https://hub.maf.org/memorial/joyce-lin-memorial

Connect: Draw near and listen to God. How is He speaking to you?

Grow: Watch the four and a half-minute video about Joyce Lin. Discuss today's theme with your wingman. How are you inspired by Joyce Lin's story?

Live: Where will you go, what will you do, and whom will you serve? How will you live today?

Prayer: (From David Holsten, MAF President & CEO) - Lord, I am grateful that you call us to participate in Your work around the world. Thank You for uniquely shaping me to serve You. Help me to have the courage to go where You want me to go and to do what You want me to do. Please help me to be sensitive to Your Word and the people You have brought into my life to guide and instruct me. I want my life to bring glory to You as I reflect Your character to others. Amen.

My response:

Connect

Grow

Live

Afterword

Now that you've finished 40 days of *Why God?*, my prayer is for you to continue reading His word with a new interest and regard for His faithfulness. He wants to be known and understood, acknowledged, trusted, and honored. I believe making Him Lord takes repeated effort. It's not a one-and-done endeavor.

Read His scriptures and connect with Him. Every day. Find a Bible-reading plan. Repeat over time. You will grow. I'm reading (for the third time in five years) the *Bible in One Year* plan from Nicky Gumbel at Holy Trinity Brompton, London. No, I'm not Anglican, but that's okay. I downloaded the app from YouVersion.

Find a Bible-teaching church and plug in. If they teach stale religion over relationship with God, go somewhere new. Finding a local church family to share life with remains one of the Lord's most exhilarating treasures. God will be faithful to lead you to the right congregation if You ask Him.

Prayer Prompts (use themes resonating with you):

A—Abide, Acknowledge, Afresh, Awaken

N—Need, Near, Next, New

G—Grace, Grow, Gratitude, Gentle, Guide

E—Eternal, Everlasting, Engage, Ears

L—Live, Love, Listen, Life

S—Steadfast, Speak, Stay, Spark

As you grow, you change. Change includes making faith your own. Not of your family, parents, friends, husband, wife, teacher, but your own. Go down the path of experiencing what some describe as a crisis of faith. During the past 40 days, I've provided numerous examples and stories to illustrate the scriptures to reflect upon, pray about, and talk over with a wingman. As you change, your attention and focus moves away from yourself to others. God wants to use you to serve in His kingdom. I hope now you understand why to choose Him.

The most humbling part of being an author and thought leader is receiving feedback. If you have made a decision to receive or re-dedicate your life to Christ, please tell me about it. If you want to share thoughts about *Why God?*, have ideas for new projects, or simply want to learn more about my platform, I'm at wxrks.co

Now it's up to you, my friend.

Go.

Live.

About the Author

Dr. Mitch Morrison currently serves as an Associate Professor and Associate Dean of Liberty University's School of Aeronautics in Lynchburg, Virginia. Captain Morrison retired from the Coast Guard in 2015 after logging 6,800 flying hours as a military aviator over 30+ years. He served in various leader roles including the Coast Guard's Deputy Director of Health, Safety, Work-Life and Chief of Aviation Safety. Dr. Morrison earned a Ph.D. in Business Administration, Master of Aeronautical Science, and Bachelor of Professional Aeronautics degrees. Mitch is also a FAA-certified helicopter and airplane flight instructor and FAA-rated helicopter Airline Transport Pilot.

Dr. Morrison's specialty areas include leader transformation, learner discipleship, and researcher. He has presented at conferences on the topics of error recognition, interdisciplinary learning, and safety leadership/culture. In 2013, he wrote *Teamworks: Transforming Health Care's Error-Prone Culture.*

In addition to his military and academic roles, Mitch has led various ministries as a trustee/elder chairman, life group leader, communion facilitator, and worship team keyboardist. Mitch is a board director for Mission Safety International, a non-profit team supporting flying safety for Christian missionary organizations since 1983. Mitch and his wife Elizabeth have been married for 28 years and live in Forest, Virginia. The Morrisons have four children: Cam, Hunter, Spencer, and Bethany.

Mitch is a certified Five Capitals coach and founder and CEO of Wxrks LLC.

You can reach Mitch at: wxrks.co

Connect. Grow. Go.